MW00783795

The New Mediterranean

Homes and Interiors Under
the Southern Sun

gestalten

Table of Contents

26

From the High Atlas Mountains to Our Living Rooms

62

Revisiting Tradition: A New Direction in Materiality

74

Sarah Ellison: An emerging furniture designer creates Mediterranean-inspired pieces for the Australian home.

98

Weaving a Mediterranean Sensibility into the Home

110

Serge Castella: Art, artifacts and archeology define the sumptuous, antique-filled homes by the French-born, Spain-based interior designer.

A Sunny
Disposition

Three continents, 23 countries, and a rich history of cultural exchange and trade going back millennia, the influence of the Mediterranean region is felt globally—and the home is no exception. When it comes to the interiors inspired by this part of the world, the storied history of the Mediterranean is evident.

There's a pervading idea that life is good in the Mediterranean. That it is all sea, sun, and siestas, plump olives and good wine. A place many of us only experience when we are on holiday. But there is more to it than that. This is a place with a way of life that is defined by its dramatic landscapes, a rich history, and a glorious climate.

Homes situated on this slice of the earth are designed to make the most of their surroundings. Stone, marble, and terracotta are extracted from the landscape and expertly shaped to suit everyday needs. Living spaces spread seamlessly between indoors and out. The terrace is critical. Furniture, woven from natural materials, is designed to be lower and longer, inviting the sitter to kick back and relax.

As Dimitris Karampatakis of architectural practice K-Studio says on page 149, at the heart of the Mediterranean aesthetic is a sense of craftedness. The unrushed nature imbued in handmade objects. The imperfections and truthfulness that are visible in the materials. Craft has been part of the cultural heritage of this region for thousands of years, with woven baskets, rustic textiles, and pottery connecting spaces to the ancient civilizations that were here before.

This is a story that is no longer limited to a single geography. In fact, many projects in this book are thousands of miles from the Med: in southern locations such as Australia, California, and Brazil, but also in places like New York and Copenhagen. The Mediterranean sensibility echoes itself in these locales through a variety of reasons, be it former colonial influences, a similar sunny climate, or simply an appreciation for the Mediterranean way of life.

Much of the Mediterranean aesthetic's widespread influence is down to our hyper-connected world. Sarah Ellison, a furniture designer profiled on pages 74–79, found inspiration underfoot on a holiday in Italy. She returned to Australia with a camera roll full of what she referred to as "tile moments." Recognizing the similarity in coastal lifestyles, her own beachy collection of tiles echoes the sun-drenched palette she saw in Italy, but expressed with her own Australian spin. Her rattan consoles and linen armchairs feel as at home in her native Byron Bay as they would on a Greek Island.

After years of stark minimalist interiors, *The New Mediterranean* asks, why not bring that joyful sense of warmth and a slower pace of life into our everyday? Why not create spaces that remind us of summer vacation—of long, languid days that stretch late into the night? It is a good question. Why not? In our increasingly digital world and the machine-cut precision of the objects that surround us, these spaces evoke salty air and sandy toes. In our high-octane urban lifestyles, *The New Mediterranean* can teach us a thing or two about slowing down—no matter where in the world we might be.

Simple Glamour of the 1960s and 1970s

The swimming pool seating area mixes rattan chairs, hammocks, and macramé plant holders.

The whitewashed house was built to recall the glamour of the 1960s and 1970s, and reflects the curvature of distant hills.

This whitewashed home on the Greek Island of Mykonos was built to suit the topography and weather conditions of the island by the owners, jewelry designer Diane Kordas and her husband, Steve Kordas. Designed by London-based architectural and interior design practice Hubert Zandberg Interiors, Zandberg says the inside was inspired by the "1960s and the 1970s, when Mykonos was a glamorous destination for Jackie Kennedy Onassis, and other Greece-bound personalities of the time. We therefore decided on a combination of barefoot glamour, simple, natural elements, and injections of retro." The home is a light, elegant, and functional space, with an outdoor dining area that has views of the pool and sea, featuring exterior furniture from Gandia Blasco. The vintage and collector pieces spread throughout the house were locally sourced, including an overhead chandelier reminiscent of beams of light. The bedroom linen is typical of Greece, combining blue and white geometric patterns, while the living room has animal skin rugs and plenty of deep, comfortable seating, framed by metallic side lamps.

Villa Agave

←|
Exterior furniture from
Gandia Blasco populates
the outdoor dining area.

↑

The living room brings the
outside inside, with cactus
trees, aloe vera plants, and
a glass-topped coffee table
built out of a tree trunk.

←

Magnificent views of the
sea are framed by the arched
entrance hallway.

↗
An external wood burner
makes for the perfect
barbecue area for outdoor
dining.

↑
The living room combines
several signature objects,
including a lacquered
replica of the face of David
by Michelangelo, a 1960s
French stool, and an
African rug.

→
Gabriel Escámez collects
a wide array of ceramic
pieces.

The Pendulum of History

Mixing materials and cultural references, art director and interior designer Gabriel Escámez's apartment in Cubelles, outside of Barcelona, brings together an array of artworks with unique objects—with wood, woven fabrics, ceramics, brass, and marble all contrasting. As the artistic director of Cobalto Studio, Escámez describes his interest in history as being like a pendulum that swings between different periods. A 1970s Mediterranean style defines the living room, which includes a lacquered replica of the face of David by Michelangelo, complemented by an African rug, French stool from the 1960s, and a small cubist painting sourced from Paris. The benches and base of the dining room table were built-in using plaster and brick, with chairs by Pierre Jeanneret, while the bathroom has a Roca sink, black marble bathtub, and an ebony bust from Africa. With the kitchen's work area made from a single trunk of dark wenge wood, the countertop is of Macael marble, which has a rough finish to make it appear as if being directly transferred from a quarry.

↑
Brick and plaster were the
materials used for the dining
room table, with chairs by
Pierre Jeanneret.

↗ →
The kitchen uses Macael
marble, complemented by
a built-in seating area with
pale woven cushions.

Home of Gabriel Escámez

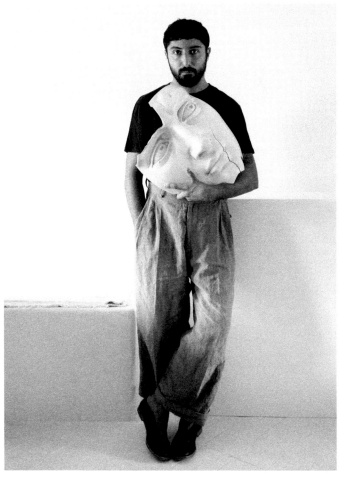

Beachside Minimalism

At a cozy $51\,m^2$ ($550\,ft^2$), this north Sydney apartment with sea views, designed by Olivia Bossy, combines the illusion of space with modernist elegance, taking cues from Eileen Gray's E-1027 house and Georgia O'Keeffe's Ghost Ranch. Bright and white, it has low-lying beds, lattice wardrobes, and an indoor rock garden inspired by Bossy's uncle who has a house in Havana. Light penetrates everywhere—the kitchen walls have been knocked down to make room for a small dining area, and the bathroom extends into the living room via a sculptural curve topped with a glass window. Bossy emphasized that the furniture "needed to work almost as a functional sculpture in its own right as I was wary of overcrowding the tiny space." As such, built-in Marrakesh plaster seating molds into the walls and converts into a single bed, alongside an S533 cantilever chair by Mies van der Rohe and wavy lamp by fellow early twentieth-century designer Eileen Gray. The space also has rattan and oak joinery, and the walls are plastered rather than painted, bringing warmth and tactility into the entire home.

←
This bedside bench com-
bines vintage objects,
from lamps to pots and
photographs.

↑
The lounge of this home
combines built-in seating
with an indoor garden and
floor tiles by Winckelmans.

→   17

↖
The children's bedroom has a custommade floor bed decorated with striped linens.

←
The lounge area has Marrakesh plaster seating that molds into the walls and converts into a single bed.

→
An indoor rock garden was inspired by Olivia Bossy's uncle, who has a house in Havana.

Freshwater

← In the entryway is a custom-made rattan and oak wardrobe by Olivia Bossy.

↓ A sculptural curve topped with a glass window extends the bathroom into the living room, making use of the daylight in every room.

Home of
Melissa Young

Anza Borrego Desert,
California, USA

Design by Melissa Young
of My Studio ID

Haçienda Home

↑
Woven fabrics are combined
with sheepskin and complemented by solid wood
furnishings.

→
The external seating area
is dotted with cacti, while
elsewhere there is an outdoor kitchen and shower
overlooking the desert
landscape.

Home of Melissa Young

This haçienda-style home in the Anza Borrego Desert combines furs, leathers hides, and woven fabrics with white and terracotta-colored walls, brick flooring, and solid wood furnishings. Together this has the effect of mixing the desert landscape with the mood of the Mediterranean. Owner, Melissa Young, the creative director of hospitality design firm MY Studio ID, was interested in creating balance by mixing styles that combined the vintage with the contemporary, and the masculine with the feminine. The house has been restored to its original style, with 46 centimeter-thick walls, hand-laid brick, laid-in sand floors and ceilings with beams of hand-hewn plank wood. The 42 interior doors were sandblasted to their original rough wood, while the living room's built-in fireplace and Moroccan-style seating blend into the architecture itself. Both an outdoor kitchen and shower look out into the rolling desert hills and arid landscape. The five bedrooms include four-poster beds and woven fabrics, as well as perfectly appointed fireplaces to warm those cold desert nights.

←
The Mediterranean mixes with Moroccan in the living room's built-in seating and fireplace.

→
The bedrooms all feature four-poster beds, woven fabrics, and fireplaces.

From the High Atlas Mountains to Our Living Rooms

In an increasingly digitized world, the handmade charm of Berber rugs injects much-needed tactility into home interiors.

→
A vintage rug, part of Laith & Leila's Desert Escape collection, photographed at the Berber Lodge just outside Marrakesh.

From the High Atlas Mountains to Our Living Rooms

Weaving has been intrinsic to the culture of the seminomadic Berber peoples of North Africa for centuries. Their rugs and tapestries thrive on imperfections, with crooked lines and asymmetrical compositions that are both geometric and soulful, minimalist and lively.

Traditionally Berber rugs were made by women deftly weaving tapestries from wool or recycled textiles at home, with little changing from generation to generation, while the men were working outdoors tending to sheep and goat herds. It was not until around the 1920s that European tastes evolved and decided that these traditional weaves were now "modern."

Le Corbusier is credited with turning the heads of his fellow modernists to Berber weaving traditions. He used Beni Ourain carpets when he designed Villa La Roche in Paris in 1923–25. There are several rugs of the same tradition on the floor of Villa Mairea, Alvar Aalto's rural retreat in Finland, and a photo taken in 1938 of Frank Lloyd Wright's Fallingwater in Pennsylvania shows yet another.

The Beni Ourain people are thought to have lived in the Atlas Mountains from the ninth century AD, and the name refers to 17 Berber tribes who primarily live there. The thick pilewoven, cream-colored rugs are traditionally made from the wool of the ancient breed of Beni Ourain sheep and have thin black lines crisscrossing to form a diamond shape. "That symbol is actually an 'X' to symbolize peace and harmony," explains Amy Elad-Echariti, the founder of the Marrakesh-based homewares label Laith & Leila. Elad-Echariti, who married into a family of Berber weavers, works directly with craftspeople across Morocco to champion their craftsmanship.

Beni Ourain rugs are traditionally made by women with no formal training and are woven from memory. Often improvised and asymmetrical, in the context of an austere, modernist interior they provide much-needed warmth. In the High Atlas Mountain region, where Mount Toubkal stands as the highest peak in North Africa, they were traditionally used as blankets and shawls. "One of the weavers I know, Miriam, puts her rug over her shoulders like a robe when she wakes up in the morning," says Elad-Echariti.

↑ ↓
London-based designer Ella Jones works with Moroccan craftspeople to produce her own designs—a geometric interpretation of the traditional. The rugs pictured on this page follow the Azilal style.

"Beni Ourain rugs are traditionally made by women with no formal training and are woven from memory."

The renewed interest in traditional textiles is certainly not limited to those coming from Morocco. Pictured here is a tapestry by Nåde, which works with Zapotec women near Oaxaca, Mexico.

←
Likewise, Pampa is an Australian studio working with makers in rural Argentina.

Although these styles of rugs are the most commonly used in western households—"people gravitate towards them because they're so minimalist," Elad-Echariti explains—they are only one strand in a diverse weaving tradition that spans throughout Morocco. This rich heritage of weaving traditions diversifies based on climate, availability of wool, and the natural materials that are available to dye the wool.

The rugs from the Azilal region of the Atlas Mountains are quite a bit more expressive. Using the same creamy wool as the Beni Ourain, the free-moving abstractions and crawling patterns are dense with symbolism. Each rug tells its own story. "They incorporate symbols like the Hand of Fatima or an evil eye for protection," says Elad-Echariti. The tints of wool are dyed using locally available plants and berries.

Comparatively, the Boucherouite rugs are a more universal weave and not necessarily attributed to any one Berber group. "These are one of the few rugs that don't use wool," says Ella Jones, founder of east London boutique A New Tribe, which sells rugs sourced from Morocco and produced in direct collaboration with Berber weavers. "Instead, they use recycled textiles. These are made all over the country and come from areas where it's not as easy to get hold of wool." Jones has been working with Berber weavers ever since she started her own rug brand, The Rug Trade, in 2013. She goes to Morocco twice a year to work with the weavers and buy rugs. "I buy way too much," she says, laughing. "Last time I bought 60 rugs when I was meant to buy 40."

When Jones started her business, it was with the intention of working with Moroccan weavers to produce pieces that she designed. "I wanted them to feel like Moroccan rugs but a contemporary version, without looking too literal," she says. "There are so many rugs out there, I don't want to redesign something that already exists."

As with any creative partnership, there were growing pains. The weavers Jones works with do not use measurements, instead doing everything by eye. "It's happened that I've given them the designs, but because they don't use measurements when they're weaving, they did the design and realized it needed to be half a meter longer, so they just wove half a meter of plain rug on the other end," she says.

Whereas more and more people are gravitating towards the improvised charm and rich color palette of these pieces, others are concerned that the tradition, craftsmanship, and narrative associated with Berber weaving is getting lost. Western demand for this style of weaving has skyrocketed, impacting both design and production. Where previously only natural materials were used to dye wool, the lexicon has expanded to include synthetically dyed fluoro pinks and neon greens. "A few people are outsourcing production of these rugs to India and they are imported back to Morocco," says Elad-Echariti.

As a result, a lot of vendors are looking to vintage Berber rugs. Jones sells a collection dating back to the 1960s that have aged beautifully, fading and flattening with time. Vintage rugs from the Beni Ourain peoples will never be wider than about two meters, made from looms that had to be portable for a nomadic people (since the 1970s, many of the tribes have settled).

→
The Rug Trade, a London-based brand working with Moroccan artisans, specializes in Boucherouite and Azilal rugs.

↓
Brands like Pampa work with artisans around the world to preserve traditional ways of making and to ensure sustainable, fair trade standards are met.

As craftspeople churn out rugs to meet global demand, Jones speculates that vintage rugs will become ever more precious. "But then the new rugs will eventually become vintage," she adds.

Social enterprise is positively impacting local dynamics, for example via Moroccan lifestyle brands that are often founded by westerners. Laith & Leila, which is named after the Arabic words for "lion" and "night," supports NGOs in North and West Africa to further education and literacy programs. According to Elad-Echariti, because they don't rely on a middleman, they can pay their weavers two to three times above average, in turn allowing the weavers to send their children to better schools and improve their living situations.

Buying a Berber rug requires some research. For those lucky enough to make it to Morocco to buy firsthand, Elad-Echariti suggests examining pieces for their quality. If the price feels cheap, it's probably not authentic. Outside urban centers in smaller cities such as Essaouira or in villages in the Atlas Mountains, rugs are more likely to be high quality. "But I wouldn't write off the vendors in the Marrakesh medina because there are a lot that are just amazing, doing hands-on work with the weavers," says Elad-Echariti.

"There are so many rugs out there, I don't want to redesign something that already exists."

> "Because Berber rugs are often dense with narrative, they can be part of a larger story within a space."

↑
Rugs featuring traditional geometric forms by Pampa.

↓
Vintage Moroccan rugs are especially favored for their beautifully faded appearance.

Before deciding on a rug, Jones recommends considering the room it will live in. "Moroccan rugs are great as they often have small highlight colors within them," she says. "So it can be really nice to pull out one of these colors and draw on this by adding more pieces of this same color to the space."

The thick, white wool Beni Ourain rugs tend to work best outside of high-traffic areas of the home. Equally, recycled Boucherouite are really playful and easy to clean, making them perfect for children's bedrooms.

Because Berber rugs are often dense with narrative, they can be part of a larger story within a space. "It's great to complement Berber rugs with smaller decorative objects that are collected on travels or over a longer period of time, so that these also tell a story and have a real connection to the owner," Jones considers.

It takes anywhere from several days to weeks or months to weave a rug by hand, depending on the size and complexity of the design. In her experiences visiting Berber homes, Elad-Echariti says it's rare to see them on the floor. "They don't really use it as a rug like we do, but they would put it up on their walls." With the time and knowledge that go into the making of each rug, it doesn't seem amiss to hang a Berber rug on the wall instead of placing it on the floor—after all, it gives an even better vantage point from which to admire the generations of knowledge and craft that have gone into creating this work of art.

→
A Pampa rug draped amidst the landscape that inspired it.

From the High Atlas Mountains to Our Living Rooms

Fruits of the Loom

Handwoven textiles can soften even the starkest space. Here, a tapestry of contemporary brands update weaving traditions.

A figure reminiscent of an Egyptian hieroglyph slam dunks a basketball. Elsewhere, Lisa Simpson gives a stoic stare. The blankets, throws, and cushions by _BFGF_, a brand by Los Angeles-based artist Lilian Martinez, deserve a second glance. Her dust-hued compositions, which feature human forms, Grecian columns, and tropical plants all tickled by contemporary references, manage to weave together the old and the new into something altogether unexpected.

Another Los Angeles-based artist weaving contemporary references into textiles is the Australian-born Mark Hendrick, founder of _Slowdown Studio_. The pieces are the result of collaborations with artists from around the world, including tropical dreamscapes by Uruguayan artist Maite García and the playful primary colors of Berlin-based illustrators Zebu. Each blanket is made from 100 percent American-grown cotton and is woven in North Carolina.

Over in New York, the latest collection of _Cold Picnic_, Hide, is inspired by one of the founder's grandfather's zebra skin, which was laid out on the floor of his home. Playful illustrations of wild animals splayed out like hunting trophies are woven into their rugs, blankets, and throws. Best of all, no zebras were hurt in the process.

_MA_ was founded by a Mexican artist looking to combine her contemporary art background with ancestral artisanal techniques. Working with native weavers, the rugs tell stories of local landscapes and folklore through pleasing geometric patterns and warm, abstract compositions. See also the characterful ceramics, where each mug is painted with a face inspired by spiritual traditions from the Sierra Madre de Oaxaca.

Located in Chattanooga, Tennessee, _Nåde_ is a small-batch textile studio where everything is made by hand and dyed using plants and food waste. Black beans, it turns out, create a cloudy shade of gray when introduced to natural wool, while warp threads achieve a rusty red from avocado pits. Nåde's wall hangings are a fringed delight, while the cushions and rugs are geometric

Cheeky textiles blending classical and contemporary references by BFGF.

Tigmi Trading imports new and vintage rugs from Morocco to their boutique in Byron Bay.

and joyful, woven at the Vida Nueva women's cooperative in Oaxaca, Mexico.

Farther south in Argentina, a team of weavers is working fastidiously using traditional looms. Their rugs can take up to six weeks to complete before winding up as part of the artisan collection of _Pampa_. The pattern of each rug is inspired by legends and the weaver's natural surroundings, and each collection takes its name from the Argentinian landscapes.

Handwoven rugs age beautifully. This is imminently clear from just a cursory glance at the vintage rugs available through the online shop and studio of _Tigmi Trading_ in Byron Bay. Dating back to the 1950s and 1960s and across Morocco, Turkey, and everywhere in between, these beautifully crafted pieces are both timeworn and timeless. These are one-of-a-kind pieces—when they are gone, they are gone.

As a counterpoint to factory-produced imitation rugs, which often mimic traditional weavings using synthetic materials, _Unicef Market_ is an online portal to richly patterned, handmade pieces coming from Mexico, the Andes, Central America, and India, sourced to a high standard of fair trade and socially responsible producers. Proceeds from purchases go towards helping children in some of the world's most vulnerable communities.

Nåde's geometric textiles are made by Mexican artisans.

"It's great to complement rugs with decorative objects that are collected on travels or over a longer period of time, so that these tell a story and have a real connection to the owner."

Blown Away

This Moroccan house made by architects Studio KO sits a little inland from Essaouira, a blustery beach town with views of the Atlantic Ocean. The L-shaped infinity pool is studded with canary-yellow sun loungers and seemingly edges into the arid landscape. With raw sandy-colored stone throughout, this structure's neutral tones are complemented by brightly colored furnishings and textiles.

↑
The structure of this home is made from sandy-colored stone throughout, which is complemented by brightly colored furnishings.

→
The living room's cast-concrete couch has cushions by Maison de Vacances, Hay, and Soufiane Zarib, with mid-century seating including a DCW chair by Eames.

"I wanted to keep it all very simple, using primarily stone, concrete, and wood beams," says Dutch designer Willem Smit. During roasting hot summers, the rooms are kept cool by the ceiling fans. Statement light fixtures include lever-arch lamps, overhead lanterns, and a Greta Magnusson Grossman Grasshopper lamp. Bedrooms feature richly colored striped bedspreads and the bathrooms have luxurious roll-top baths. The living room's mainstay is a woodburning fireplace, next to which a vast column of wood is neatly stacked. Here, a cast-concrete couch is fitted with cushions by Maison de Vacances, Hay, and Soufiane Zarib; mid-century seating includes a DCW chair by Eames—all, needless to say, comfortable as well as effortlessly stylish.

← Richly colored striped blankets cover the beds, contrasting with the sandy stonewalls.

↓ Canary-yellow sun loungers rest next to the L-shaped infinity pool, with views of Essaouira.

Previous page:
Left: The kitchen's statement light fixtures include Anglepoise lamps and overhead lanterns.

Right: A woodburning fireplace, next to which wood is neatly stacked.

| Villa Mabrouka

Villa Mabrouka

Floating Above the Sea

Designed by Stockholm-based firm One of a Kind Architects (OOAK), this minimalist summer house is akin to a single-story geometric object balanced upon the rocky cliffs of Karpathos Island in Greece beneath the blue Mediterranean sky. A quiet retreat for a Paris-based, French-Swedish couple who love to windsurf, the vast windows of this structure frame the Aegean Sea. The reinforced concrete building has skylights and wooden doors, a series of different voids blurring the limits between inside and out, connecting the house with large terraces. At the core of the building is a large courtyard, sheltering the space from strong Karpathian winds. In the minimally decorated dining room, ceramic plates are mounted on the wall above a pale wooden table and chairs. White plaster and polished stone create soft interior surfaces, and the green kitchen cabinets and island provide rare moments of color. These sit alongside elegant Scandinavian furniture and splashes of colorful woven textiles.

← The kitchen cabinets provide moments of green in an otherwise soft and light interior of white, referencing traditional Karpathian architecture.

↑ This reinforced concrete building balances upon the rocky cliffs of Karpathos Island in Greece, cantilevered with Vierendeel trusses.

↑
Magnificent views of the
Mediterranean Sea are
visible from the living room.
The Scandinavian furniture
and colorful woven textiles
are complemented by the
woodburning stove.

↗
Ceramic plates adorn the
dining room's walls by
the pale wooden table and
chairs.

← →
Wooden doors and skylights
flood the reinforced structure with light, while the
inside and outside spaces
are connected by large
terraces.

| Maison Kamari | Paros Island, Greece | Design by Re-act Architects in collaboration with Alexandra Leroux and Damien de Medeiros |

Cubic Cycladic Comfort

↑

Set on the Greek Island of Paros, Maison Kamari is an exemplar of Cycladic architecture, consisting of a series of white interlocking cubes surrounded by olive trees and mountains.

→

The living room has a pinewood stool by Charlotte Perriand and another stool from 1930s Burkina Faso, and vintage lamps.

Maison Kamari, a summer home by the fishing village of Aliki on the Greek Island of Paros, is an exemplar of Cycladic architecture. The idyllic house consists of a series of white interlocking cubes, surrounded by olive trees and mountains. The pool is connected to the terrace by a wide concrete staircase, while another leads up to the structure's flat roof, where you can admire the panoramic view. Inside, the owners Alexandra Leroux and Damien de Medeiros sourced mid-century pieces from markets in Athens, Paros, and Paris. Intimacy, coziness, and comfort are key. In the living room, the smooth curves of two 1950s rattan chairs by Dirk van Sliedregt sit next to a pinewood stool by French designer Charlotte Perriand and another 1930s vintage one sourced from Burkina Faso. Two chunky dark wood coffee tables contrast with the sofa's natural fibers. Each bedroom has an ensuite bathroom, while the open-plan kitchen is decorated with baskets from Zimbabwe.

Maison Kamari

←
An olive tree grown inside
the courtyard, observed by
a lone yellow chair.

↑
A 1950s rattan chair by
Dirk van Sliedregt decorates
the living room.

↗
Each bedroom has an
ensuite bathroom with
sunbeam mirrors and
wooden stools.

→
The kitchen is decorated
with wall-mounted baskets
from Zimbabwe.

Artful Living

This home comprises a
strong geometric structure
surrounded by cactus plants.

In the hallway, soil vessels
by Raya Stefanova rest
on a solid wood plinth;
nearby stand welded-steel
sculptures and a Ethiopian
chief's chair.

↑
Soft neutral fabrics define
the living room, from the
white wall hanging to the
sofa, cushions, and woven
rug. A Shoji paper lantern
hangs over a low table,
both by Faye Toogood.

→
The earthy textured walls
of the bathroom contrast
with the smooth finish of
the bath, which from afar
appears to float.

→
Above the bed hangs
a bamboo pendant by
Ay Illuminate and a huge
mixed-media artwork by
Faye Toogood on the wall,
framed by floating side
tables.

This geometric structure is unassuming from the outside, with
sandy white walls and cactus plants framing a home filled with
modernist art and design. The house was designed by Faye
Toogood, who was inspired by the "spirit of her grandmother."
She used a muted color palette of white and beige tones, and
a feeling of warmth is introduced via a chunky wood plinth in
the hallway. On this different sculptures sit next to nearby tall
totems, as well as woven lampshades, and fabric wall drapes.
Thick wooden beams support the ceilings throughout—this is
a rustically elegant Spanish villa. The dining room, hung with
large-scale monochrome abstracts, leads to a magnificent
balcony that looks onto the sea. By contrast, in the bedroom
a huge white abstract painting sits above the bed, beneath
which wall-mounted lamps illuminate floating side tables.
Piles of wood are stacked by the living room's feature fireplace,
alongside which a huge sofa begs to be stretched out upon—
the perfect vantage point from which to soak up the splendor.

| Can Cardell | Palma de Mallorca, Spain | Design by Moredesign |

Modern Traditions in Mallorca

↑ →

Sandy-colored stones comprise the three-tiered exterior of this home. The terrace, which has turrets like a Spanish fort, features lights hanging from a trellis handmade from tree branches.

Magnificent seascapes and verdant countryside surround this home in Palma de Mallorca, which has huge French windows to soak up the view. Designed by architects Oro del Negro and Manuel Villanueva, founders of studio Moredesign, they describe their "passion for craftsmanship, creativity, tactile, and natural materials, and a lived-in sensibility" in their aesthetic ethos. The sandy-colored walls of the three-tiered exterior of the property were preserved, while the interior was completely redone. The terrace even kept its turrets that are reminiscent of a Spanish fort. Using old wood, marble, lime, and river pebbles, a connection was created between inside and outside, traditional Mallorcan style mixed with the more modern. The whitewashed living room combines hanging baskets with a mix of wooden furnishings and neutral fabrics. Ocher-colored cushions in the seating niche by the kitchen match the lamp and ceramics collection, which was amassed in markets all over the world. The kitchen uses marble plaster, bleached wood, and a sink made of carved limestone, as well as brass fittings, while the bedrooms have patterned bedspreads found in London's flea markets.

→

Can Cardell

|←
Patterned cushions, throws, and bedspreads are made from woven textiles in earthy shades of ocher, brown, red, and apricot.

↑
Hanging plants decorate the living room and mix with wooden furnishings and neutral fabrics, as well as a ceramics collection sourced from markets internationally.

←
Old wood, marble, lime, and river pebbles are the materials used throughout the house, not least in the bathroom, which has a deep trough sink reminiscent of a farmhouse.

Revisiting Tradition: A New Direction in Materiality

In the Mediterranean region, a renewed interest in traditional local materials and building techniques is inspiring a modern take on sustainable architecture, one with a foot in the past and an eye on the future.

→
Traditional Moroccan mud brick with contemporary updates.

Revisiting Tradition: A New Direction in Materiality

↗
In the case of Casa Modesta, the architect's grandfather's home was renovated into a nine-room hotel. The reimagined form reinterprets traditional techniques and materials in a contemporary space.

When Portuguese architect Vânia Brito Fernandes completed the refurbishment of Casa Modesta, turning her grandfather's former house in the Algarve into a nine-room hotel, it didn't look that different to how it looked when it was built in the 1940s. In fact, it didn't look that different from houses in that region dating back much further.

Casa Modesta is a prototype for a new direction in architecture spearheaded by Fernandes and her Lisbon-based firm, Par. Taking its cues from a sixteenth-century architectural movement called "arquitectura chã" (meaning plain architecture), Fernandes calls this new direction "casa chã." "With casa chã we try to reinterpret the architectural culture and traditional construction knowledge, but with a contemporary logic," she says. In other words, constructing buildings the way they would have been in the past, but re-thought to suit contemporary life.

As architects are grappling with the task of designing sustainable buildings, they're left with a need to innovate. Many architects are looking ahead by looking to the past, gleaning knowledge from traditional construction techniques and celebrating the use of local materials. Lisbon-based architect João Gameiro agrees with Fernandes's approach. He likens this movement to the same trend we see in food: "People want to eat less processed food. We're also interested in less processed architecture with less processed materials."

Our farm-to-fork interest in where our food comes from—and how far it had to travel to reach us—can also be thought of in architectural terms. "Traditional knowledge is related to sustainable practices, sustainable ways of building, and the use of local materials," Gameiro continues. In the Mediterranean, this looks like new stone buildings that resemble older structures, and old buildings that have been stripped back to reveal original floorboards, timberbeam ceilings and aging plaster walls. The more layers of history, the better. Let old buildings be old buildings. "There are a lot of techniques like working with clay and materials that people had been using for centuries that are now coming back into use," Gameiro says. "They were forgotten and disused because they were thought not to be modern enough."

Casa Modesta is a good example of this. The refurbishment retains the building's historic texture, while the new extensions are built following the vocabulary of the region's architecture. The building uses only local stone, found in a quarry a few kilometers away. Brass details are used throughout to add a sense of refinement to the otherwise traditional palette. Everything has a purpose, with no superfluous flourishes. The floor is made from terracotta tiles, one of the oldest building materials in the world, favored especially by the Romans.

With this building, Fernandes echoes "arquitectura chã," which spread following the death

→
Architect João Gameiro
created the terrazzo flooring
at this apartment in Lisbon
using geometric marble
offcuts to form a seemingly
random pattern.

↓
The Lapa Apartment follows
the Pombaline style of
Portuguese architecture
from the eighteenth century.
Where possible, the apartment maintains its historic
texture.

in1521 of King Manuel, whose reign is marked by its many opulent late-Gothic buildings. "Portugal spent a lot of money on architecture," she says. After the king's death, the backlash was structures built simply using inexpensive materials found nearby. "They did what they needed, and didn't do any more, but in fact the houses were very good."

If one steps back to look at the Mediterranean region as a whole, the architecture in these countries isn't always easy to define. Like language and food, it depends where you stand. With its many cultural groups invading one another over the centuries, new ideas spread and with them, new ways of building. But throughout the region, from Jerusalem all the way to Spain, there are similarities.

The rocky terrain you'll find throughout the region is why so many of the buildings are made from stone and not from timber like their Alpine counterparts. Thick walls are built from local stone carved out of the landscape, held together with earthen matter and coated in a white lime render, which reflects the sun. The thickness of the walls and the small openings keep the homes cool in the summer and warm in the winter. "We know that these were made in a very unprofessional

Revisiting Tradition: A New Direction in Materiality

way, a tradition that was transferred from father to son," says London-based architectural researcher Doron von Beider. "It's quite a natural style."

The Patio House overlooking the Aegean Sea on the Greek Island of Karpathos does not quite fit this description, at least not at first glance. The bunker-like concrete edifice doesn't resemble everyone's impression of a Greek summer house. But this building, too, is a story of championing local materials and the craft associated with it. The concrete block floats on its hilltop like a brutalist UFO. "Every manmade alteration would be visible in this unique lot with its jagged, textured cliffs," says Maria Papafigou, a Greek architect who is one of the partners at One of a Kind, the Stockholm-based architecture practice behind the house. "The question became how to introduce a foreign object—a house—into this spectacular landscape, enhancing its qualities without altering its character."

Because of the financial crisis happening in Greece, Papafigou was conscious to use materials that would focus on the social and economic aspect of sustainability. "We chose to use concrete mainly due to the fact that it was produced on the island and we could avoid transporting materials from elsewhere, as well as supporting the local industry," she says. It also meant they could work with an entirely local construction team, as the local builders on Karpathos are very familiar with working with concrete.

Inside, the building uses local stone on the floors, softened by woven textiles and bespoke furniture. The stone creates a path from the house all the way down to the sea. "Karpathos is also known for its ceramics so we collaborated with a Greek ceramic artist and we incorporated handmade tiles on a bench in the patio area," Papafigou continues.

She's not the only one to reference the financial crisis. Gameiro has a theory that there's a link between the crisis and the renewed interest in traditional craft. "Because there were no jobs, a lot of people had to go back to their parents' homes.

→
The exterior staircases at Casa Modesta are designed in keeping with traditional architecture in the Algarve region.

Patio House uses local stone for paving and ceramic tiles—a nod to Karpathos's ceramic industry—in addition to using concrete from the island.

→

"Rather than trying to mimic the landscape, Patio House is gently placed on the site as an object, leaving the surrounding landscape as untouched as possible," says architect Maria Papafigou.

Their parents had carpentry shops, they had ceramics, so they had these old businesses and the younger generation are learning these crafts." He suggests that countries like Portugal are starting to learn the value of their tradition. "Maybe what we've been doing the last 20 years doesn't add much cultural richness, because it's just a copy and paste of something that worked in other countries."

Gameiro explored his own approach to local craft when he returned to Portugal, after spending eight years working in London, to take on a commission for the refurbishment of an 1819 Lapa Apartment in Lisbon. The underlying aim was to preserve the "Pombalino" style of architecture, which is typical to Lisbon. It retains the fading frescoes and exposes the timber ceilings. Original features like the arch windows are retained, but updated with a contemporary black frame.

"So it's the plurality of exposing original elements and yet there is still something that keeps you from feeling like you're in a preserved, historical apartment," Gameiro says. The Lapa Apartment harmonizes old and new, but perhaps the best example of this is underfoot. Small rectangles of marble form a seemingly random pattern on the floor and are bound together by white concrete, like a Memphis-style terrazzo in a subdued palette of pink and gray. The bespoke floor was inspired by the Mediterranean tradition

"We chose to use concrete mainly due to the fact that it was produced on the island."

of reusing marble leftovers for flooring. Gameiro bought these marble pieces "for next to nothing." He continues, "You just need a craftsman to carve these pieces of marble. Most of them already came to us at a certain length because they were leftovers from another building."

When the sun shines through the windows, it lands on the marble, which catches the light. As light moves through the apartment, Gameiro's interpretation of traditional terrazzo glows, and it couldn't be a better example of how traditional techniques, sustainability, and modern design coalesce.

Surface Level

Terrazzo, tadelakt, and terracotta tiles: the natural materials to create a Mediterranean materiality.

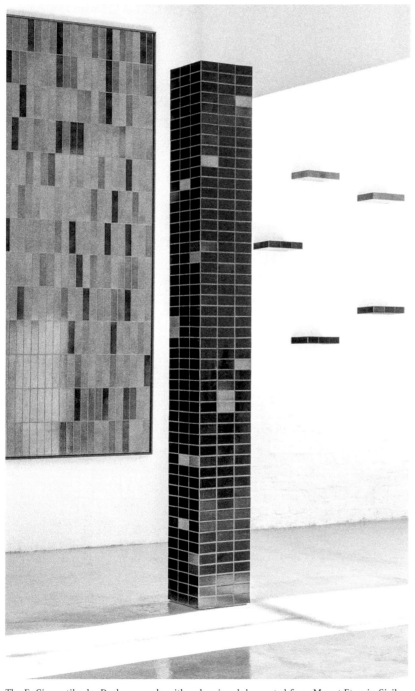

The ExCinere tiles by Dzek are made with volcanic ash harvested from Mount Etna in Sicily.

When Brent Dzekciorius and Max Lamb released Marmoreal—an aggregate of terrazzo formed of large flecks of orange, blues, and creams—the design world couldn't get enough of it. Expect the same for the follow up: after three years of experimentation London-based _Dzek_ is back with a new collaboration, this time with Amsterdam-based studio Formafantasma. ExCinere is a collection of surface tiles glazed with volcanic ash collected from Mount Etna. For Formafantasma, it's a continuation of the studio's previous exploration of volcanic ash: in 2014, they launched a furniture collection built from lava harvested following Mount Etna's eruption in 2013.

Granby Workshop from Liverpool is another studio looking at nontraditional ways of firing surfaces. Their Smoked Ceramics are a collection of handles and tiles that were smoked in a sawdust-filled barbecue for 12 hours. Other pieces include their own Granby Rock, a terrazzo-like material comprising recycled building debris, or their encaustic tiles which shine in a bright white with brushstrokes in cheerful primary colors.

Texas-based _Domingue Architectural Finishes_ picks up where traditional Mediterranean architecture leaves off, specializing in lime washes, natural plasters, and mineral paints that are applicable for both interior and exterior surfaces. The result is textural and deep, giving the impression the surface has looked like this for decades.

Another company specializing in natural plasters is the Crete-based _Minoeco_. Named after the ancient Minoans who lived on the Greek Island, Minoeco is inspired by ancient recipes for Moroccan tadelakt, lime, and clay plaster—architectural finishes that are both hard-wearing and beautiful to look at.

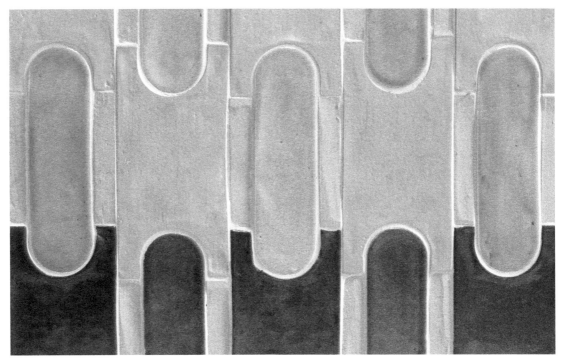

Cristina Celestino's tiles for Fornace Brioni. The ones pictured here are from the Giardino all'Italiana collection and inspired by the formality of Italian gardens.

In business since 1933, _Huguet_ is a Mallorca-based specialist of hydraulic tiles who count architects Herzog & de Meuron and David Chipperfield among their collaborators. In one of their latest collaborations, they have teamed up with Swiss designer Alfredo Häberli to create a collection that combines a rustic texture with geometric Swiss design. Their speckled washbasins deserve to be highlighted, especially the minty green terrazzo sink with an inset space for a house plant that was created in collaboration with London design studio Sella Concept.

Since 1920, _Fornace Brioni_ has worked with the historic tradition of cotto (an Italian brick tile), crafting tiles using clay harvested from the banks of the Po River. In 2017, the business enlisted Italian architect Cristina Celestino as creative director. Indeed, her work breathes new life into this heritage brand: the Mosaico collection features mini tiles in the red and gray hues of the raw materials, while the Giardino delle Delizie collection—all coral pinks, wine reds, and forest greens—is inspired by the grottoes of Renaissance gardens.

Spanish architect Patricia Urquiola's Tierras for _Mutina_ is a collection of terracotta and clay tiles that are inspired by the concept of sedimentation and Mediterranean craft traditions. The result is creamy in color, with geometric intrigue. Also for Italian brand Mutina, Urquiola has designed a terracotta room divider, "an experimentation of three-dimensional bricks."

Encaustic tiles and bowls by Granby Workshop are made from blocks of colored clay that are marbled together by hand.

"It's about reinterpreting the architectural culture and traditional construction knowledge, but with a contemporary logic."

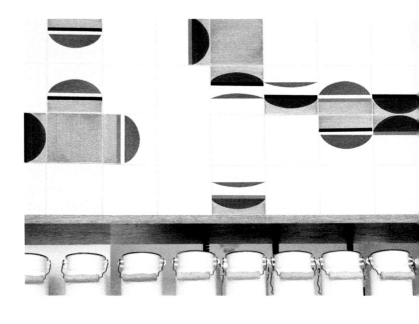

Bondi Beach may be a long way from the Mediterranean, but designer Sarah Ellison captures a southern European influence and expresses it in an unquestionably Australian way.

Sarah Ellison

It would be an understatement to say that designer Sarah Ellison has spent a lot of time looking at furniture. She spent 10 years as an interiors stylist in the fast-paced world of glossy monthlies and for every photoshoot she developed, sourced, and styled for leading interiors magazine *Real Living,* the next one was always waiting. This type of work has its benefits: a Rolodex of industry contacts and an encyclopedic knowledge of the furniture market and how people respond to it.

But it also comes with its disadvantages. At times, Ellison admits the breakneck speed at which magazines operate felt unsustainable. "I think I really yearned for a sense of permanence in my work," she says. "After 10 years I was asking myself the question, 'What's next?'"

After sourcing and styling furniture, the next logical step is to design it. "From my knowledge of the Australian interiors landscape, I felt there was a lack of brands offering original design with a high-end feeling for the average consumer." Having identified this as her niche in the market, Ellison launched Sarah Ellison Studio in 2017—today the mood she's created is a decidedly coastal Australian one, all salty air and city-side beaches, articulated through rattan and soft linen, terracotta tiles and travertine tables.

With no formal training in furniture design, Ellison let intuition lead the way. "I know what I like and I know how I want things to look and feel," she says. But beyond knowing what she wants, she also knows her customer. "They have an eye for design but still want functional and practical furniture." The studio is a team of two, but growing fast with an imminent expansion to America and then Europe soon to follow.

Three collections in, her body of work spans cozy armchairs to angular, 1970s-inspired vases, sandy-colored cushions to rattan consoles. "Wearing my stylist hat, I'm often thinking about the whole room first," she continues. "The world I want to create and the pieces I need to help create that mood."

Her premiere collection, The New Wave, is bathed in a mustardy palette of the sun setting over a blue-gray sea. "My first collection needed to be true to me, who I am, and how I live as a coast-loving Australian," she says. "Fabrics like flax linen sit next to velvets, and stones like marble are mixed with brass, bringing the raw and the refined together, a bit like the coast and the city sitting side by side."

As a former resident of Bondi Beach, a stylish Sydney suburb that brings together the city and the beach, Ellison is never far from the sea. And in turn, a coastal Australian sensibility is never far from her work.

"My aim is to craft a uniquely Australian aesthetic with an international influence." To Ellison, this is expressing her influences—which span from Italian living rooms to Moroccan walls—in a distinctly Australian way. Sometimes that means using a specific color or fabric, elsewhere this lies in the choice of materials. A defining quality for Australian interiors, she says, is about natural light. "We have a beautiful moderate climate, so a lot of design is centered around the weather."

←
Warm-colored glass and mirrored plinth boxes and vases that evoke the colors of the Australian sunset.

→
Refined brass details are a constant throughout Ellison's work. The marble-topped Stacey table is a fine example of this.

"Fabrics like flax linen sit next to velvets, and stones like marble are mixed with brass, bringing the raw and the refined together, a bit like the coast and the city sitting side by side."

Sarah Ellison

> "I knew I wanted to work with rattan as it reminded me of furniture my mother had in our home as a child."

↑
The Halston console from the Golden collection is crafted from rattan with brass details.

↗
A black powder-coated steel frame with textured linen form the ultra-cozy Alva chair, from Ellison's debut collection, The New Wave.

→
The Scallop, part of Ellison's collection with Australian tile manufacturer Teranova.

Her collection for Australian tile maker Teranova expresses these influences in yet another celebration of sand and sun. The six tile designs evoke the beach both in their names—Corfu, Cinque Terre, Scallop—and in their graphic patterns. The Cinque Terre designs are especially inspired by their namesake, with half circles and rectangles referencing the buildings and umbrellas of Monterosso in Liguria. The geometric shapes are softened by a characteristically Australian color palette, and are made from encaustic cement with a matt finish that reminds Ellison of the patina of well-worn Italian floors. "The Mediterranean is so full of inspiring and unexpected tile moments," she says. "I remember one year after a trip to the Amalfi Coast, all the photos I brought back were of tiled floors."

Her most recent collection is Golden, a series of tables, seating, and a mirror crafted from rattan. "I knew I wanted to work with rattan as it reminded me of furniture my mother had in our home as a child." She's given the straw-colored pieces an elevated edge with brass detailing and chunky proportions. The collection plays with a handmade feel and an afterglow of summer holidays. Tucked away in the southern hemisphere, it's hard not to envy Australian beachside living where days seem to be punctuated by surf breaks and avocado toast. But even if Sydney-side living might not be in the cards for all of us, Sarah Ellison's pieces tell a nostalgic story of a gentle life by the sea. It might just be the next best thing.

Sarah Ellison

Extremadura's Late-Eighteenth-Century Spanish Villa

La Hermandad de Villalba guesthouse is a late-eighteenth-century Spanish villa in the country's western Extremadura region, which is known for its wine production. Converted by architecture studio Lucas y Hernández-Gil, it once served as a home for noble families in the area, but later became the headquarters for the Franco army. Numerous original features have been emphasized including the vaulted ceilings, brick arches, and plaster moldings. The space is minimally decorated and furnished, including pattern-engraved doors painted light green and walls of pale terracotta pink, which is in fact raw lime mortar. There are three bedrooms on the second floor, which was once a larder used to dry and cure meat, while downstairs has a living room, dining room, kitchen, and cellar. Local potters created terracotta tiles for the inside flooring and the external courtyard, which contains a saltwater swimming pool. The furnace in the sitting room uses wall-mounted, deep-red glazed tiles that contrast with the matt finish of the terracotta floor tiles—both mimic the color of the town's terrain and create a sense of place.

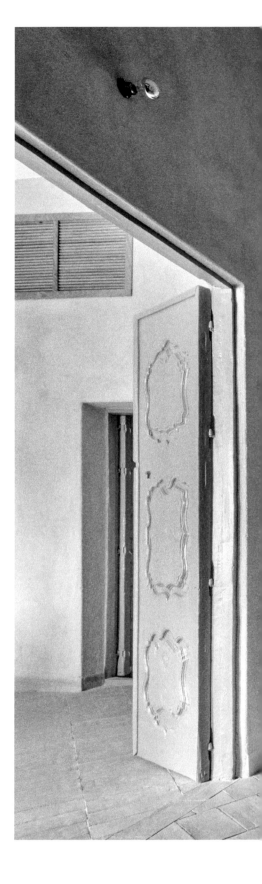

←
This late-seventeenth-century Spanish villa was historically used by both local noble families and Franco's army.

↑
Vaulted ceilings, brick arches, carved doors, and plaster moldings comprise some of the building's original features.

←
Minimally decorated, the
bedroom has raw lime mor-
tar walls and combines a
woven rug, rattan armchair,
and white linens with an
overhead lamp.

↗
Outside, the saltwater swimming pool is surrounded
by terracotta tiles made by
local potters.

↑
The lounge mixes earthy-
colored fabrics with
ceramics and woven baskets,
offset by French sculptor
Guy Bareff's sconces.

→
The pale gray of the
poured-concrete flooring
in the lobby contrasts
with the caramel-colored
suede chairs.

Hôtel Les Roches
Rouges

Saint Raphaël,
France

Design by
Festen Architecture

A Secluded Paradise

Set within the rocks of the French nature reserve Massif de l'Esterel, which is between Saint Tropez and Cannes, this late 1950s-early 1960s building was converted by Hugo Sauzay and Charlotte de Tonnac of Paris-based Festen Architecture. Inside the Hôtel Les Roches Rouges, seating uses a combination of fabrics from tan leather and caramel-colored suede to ocher cushions. The lounge has sconces by French sculptor Guy Bareff, while a marigold-hued pendant light hangs over a cozy nook. The tones of wood vary through-out, from the pale coffee tables to the rich red wood grain of the stools. The high-ceiling bedrooms are whitewashed and decorated with white linens and natural fiber rugs, with balconies featuring bright canvas chairs. The windows have been widened to afford a better perspective on the breathtak-ing sea views. Concrete floors were poured to create a vintage Mediterranean feel, with much of the furniture custommade by local French carpenters.

↑
The whitewashed suites
have high ceilings and wide
windows, combining bam-
boo chairs with chocolate-
colored rugs and bedspreads.

←
The restaurant La Plage
offers typical and season-
al Provençal dishes, with
furnishings offset by woven
baskets and terracotta
plant pots.

↗ →
The lobby's wood tones
range from the pale coffee
tables to the rich red wood
grain of the stools, much of
the furniture custommade
by local French carpen-
ters. A variety of abstract,
landscape, and figurative
art lines the walls, from
paintings to prints and
photographs.

Home of
Jonny Ribeiro

New York City, USA

Design by Jonny Ribeiro

An Art Lover's Playground

↑ →
Geometric shapes and sharp
angles define the decor
in the living room, with
stacked books, seashell
sculptures, and an eclectic
mix of styles including rustic wooden sculptures from
New York's Annex Markets.

This New York apartment is crammed full of unique art and design objects.
It has woven blue textiles and warm beige wooden flooring and furniture
throughout. And with its shell sculpture, this space has a touch of soothing
seaside warmth. Ribeiro used to source antiques for Ralph Lauren and is
interested not in the specific style of time or place, but in what one's eye is
instinctively drawn to aesthetically. Passionate about Japanese design and
Southern folk art, the bedroom combines an Isamu Noguchi ceiling lantern
and a hand-painted devil sculpture. A 1880s dry sink functions as a vast
nightstand, while a vintage Jean Prouvé replica swing light is customized
with a canonical shade. In the living room, geometric shapes and sharp
angles define the decor, a cherry-red coffee table in the middle. The rustic
wooden sculptures were bought at New York's Annex Markets, a 1960s rock
light by French designer André Cazenave and a cartoonish lithograph by
British artist Danny Fox, depicting a cowboy. This eclectic mix sums up the
mood of the place: an art lover's playground.

↑
A lithograph by Danny Fox depicts a cartoonish cowboy.

←
The living room's red coffee table has sculptures influenced by Joan Miró.

→
An Isamu Noguchi ceiling lantern and a hand-painted devil sculpture adorn the bedroom, influenced by Japanese design and Southern folk art, as well as an 1880s dry sink used as a nightstand.

Brazil's Building Blocks

↑
Patterned ceramic ventilation bricks create partitions and furniture, inspired by cobogó blocks from Brazil's buildings of the 1930s.

Designed by architect Alan Chu, this 98 m^2 (1,054 ft^2) São Paulo apartment is defined by its transparency and lightness. Using patterned ceramic ventilation bricks as partitions and furniture, as well as original bare brick walls painted white, the project is titled after the cobogó blocks that were often used in Brazil's buildings of the 1930s—materials were famously used by architects Lúcio Costa and Oscar Niemeyer. "Initially, cobogós were made of cement only," Chu explains. "With their popularization, they started to be molded with other materials such as clay, glass, ceramic, etc. The project takes advantage of this construction element by exploring function, color, graphics, and the effects of light." When the sun shines on the cobogós, they create vivid patterns. Other materials in the apartments include burnt ceramic floors and gray countertops in the bathroom and kitchen, as well as iron bars used to build units for food and crockery. Furniture ranges from rattan chairs to tables that also use cobogó blocks, uniting the apartment's aesthetic.

↑
Rattan chairs and wooden
furniture complement the
parquet flooring.

↗
Iron bars were used to build
units for food and crockery.

→
Creative tabletops made
from cobogó blocks are
complemented by a collec-
tion of terracotta pots.

Timeless Tessellations

The unique features of this
Barcelona home include
colored floor tiles and
arched doorways with inlaid
windows.

→
The living room has high
ceilings, ornate stucco
work ceilings, and molded
cornices, the multi-colored
lightshade echoed in the
bright colors of the cushions
below.

When your home is a playground of color and pattern, as designer Paloma Lanna's Barcelona apartment is, you also need moments of minimalist calm. True to Barcelona's characteristic style, tiles of every tone run throughout this space, from the deep earthy reds and ochers in the hallways to the bright blues and oranges in the living room. Lanna defines her design studio, Paloma Wool, as, "A multidisciplinary creative project that brings together artists to collaborate on the making of each collection," adding, "we remain detached from the seasons of the fashion industry." In other words: their approach to design is timeless, as is the case with this home. Furniture ranges from wicker chairs to wooden sideboards and tables nodding to 1960s Danish design, alongside hanging baskets and plants in terracotta pots that give the space luscious moments of green. Majestic doors open up each of the rooms, which have high ceilings, molded cornices, and arched windows that allow light to pour in, further illuminating the already captivating space.

↖
The minimalist bedroom
uses white linens and fabrics
for a touch of essential
elegance.

←
Homeowner Paloma Lanna's
collection of ceramics, all
with unique glazes.

↑ →
In the living room of home
owner Paloma Lanna, fur-
niture nods to 1960s Danish
design, while the artwork
is reminiscent of Matisse's
expressionistic drawings.

　　　Home of Paloma Lanna

Weaving a Mediterranean Sensibility into the Home

Rattan furniture has a rich history spanning thousands of years. Today, a growing penchant for woven furniture is helping give European wicker furniture workshops a new lease on life, with some proving to be as resilient as the material itself.

→
Part of rattan's enduring quality is that it works both indoors and outdoors.

Weaving a Mediterranean Sensibility into the Home

Every year since the early 1990s, a small gathering meets in the Provençal village of Vallabrègues to celebrate the Festival de la Vannerie (Basketry Festival). Here, the ancient art of weaving the basket willow that historically grew on the adjacent Rhône River is demonstrated live. Baskets are displayed throughout the town, piled high on horse-drawn wagons and people in period dress dance through the street. "It's a very rich heritage in this area, not around furniture but around basketry," says Benoît Rauzy, one of the three cofounders of Vallabrègues-based furniture brand Atelier Vime, which specializes in locally made wicker and rattan furniture.

No longer seen as best left in the era of 1990s patio furniture, wicker furniture is back in favor once more. In fact, the ancient craft of weaving functional objects in our lives dates back to ancient civilizations around the world—wicker was favored by the ancient Egyptians, the Victorians, and the modernists. Today, its versatility between indoor and outdoor environments, not to mention the lightweight ease of moving it between the two—makes it especially befitting to a Mediterranean home.

In addition, it ties into the growing movement around craftsmanship. "As a reaction to the wave of minimalism and focus on machine-made perfection, there has been a return to craft and an appreciation for the process of making," says Evelina Mamedovaite of London interior design practice The Studio. But where there is a revived interest in handmade pieces, the workshops to craft these pieces are experiencing decline.

Atelier Vime is one exception. Founded in 2016 when Rauzy and cofounders Anthony Watson and Raphaëlle Hanley purchased an eighteenth-century hôtel particulier, which today operates as the brand's headquarters and shoppable showroom, Rauzy says that even the building itself has a long-standing history of wicker. They found old records in the attic documenting weaving techniques, which the atelier is using today as an inspiration to revive historic methods of braiding. "It was a huge proportion of the population that was involved in this industry," explains Rauzy. This lasted until the 1970s—the last workshop in the village closed in 1972. Today, with an uncompromising approach to quality, Atelier Vime is bringing wicker-woven furniture back to Vallabrègues.

↗
The wicker floor vase and textured wood offer a rustic counterpoint to the limestone tiles at Villa Castelluccio, designed by Andrew Trotter in Italy.

↘
Wicker in the Provence region was historically tied to transporting fish and fruits. Here a wicker container is also used as a bedside table.

The first thing to know about wicker is that it's not a material. Wicker instead refers to the act of weaving natural fibers, like willow, rattan, or bamboo. The most common material for wicker furniture in Europe is the Salix viminalis, a green willow found growing in wet conditions throughout Europe and parts of Asia. In the region where

↑
A pair of mirrors made of braided rattan and brass outline, part of Atelier Vime's vintage archives.

←
A rattan chair in the Barcelona apartment of fashion designer Paloma Lanna, founder of Paloma Wool.

Atelier Vime was established, Rauzy says basketry was linked to the transport of fruits, vegetables, and fish. "So it's very linked to the Mediterranean climate and river."

Whereas the green willow plants can be sourced locally within Europe, with rattan it's a longer journey. There are more than 600 species of rattan native to the tropical forests of southeast Asia. The vine-like plant crawls up trees to reach the sunny canopy. The plant is sturdy, yet flexible and not hollow like bamboo.

"Handmade rattan furniture is extremely labor intensive," says Lulu Lytle, who is writing a book about the global history of rattan and is the creative director of Soane Britain, a furniture brand with a century-old rattan workshop. "The plant arrives in the workshops in bales and is then cut to size. The canes are soaked and then steamed to make them more malleable. Once they are soft enough to be woven, each cane is either bent into shape or woven by hand, which is rather like knitting without the needles, and a lot more physical.

As it dries, each of the rattan strands contracts, giving the piece a tight finish."

By the nineteenth century, wicker furniture was thought of as having a pastoral charm, for use in casual settings. Rattan, on the other hand, bore the allure of the exotic. Lytle says that the material came to Europe by nineteenth-century traders returning from Indonesia, China, and Japan. "As trade with the Far East increased in the eighteenth and nineteenth centuries, rattan was imported to Europe and made popular because of its strength and versatility," she says.

Its use at the beginning wasn't necessarily limited to furniture. In the nineteenth century, this abundant material—which is neither a tree nor a shrub, but a liana—was used as packing material on ships. On the long journey from China to London, for instance, rattan was used to keep the boxes of tea from thrashing about, not unlike how we use styrofoam packing peanuts today.

"You have lots of rattan furniture until after the Second World War, especially in France," says Rauzy. "Because of the lack of raw materials, people like Janine Abraham, all these postwar designers, they were using rattan because it was cheap and available." Other rattan furniture makers like Bonacina started looking at how rattan furniture could be used in collaborations with modernist designers such as Tito Agnoli.

By the late 1960s, another Mediterranean furniture brand, the Valencia-based Expormim, had furnished the influx of European tourism to Spain. Demand soared as Mediterranean beaches were lined with wicker and cane loungers. When the company noticed a shortage of local raw materials, they began importing rattan from Indonesia. Both Bonacina and Expormim are still producing furniture today.

"Rattan is most commonly used in one of two ways: as a surface treatment for room dividers, ceiling tiles, or table tops, or to create three-dimensional pieces, like sculptural pendant lights, or chairs." Interior designer Chrystal Ohoh, who is Evelina Mamedovaite's partner at The Studio, says, "Design classics like Gio Ponti's Superleggera chair, or the wicker wrapped brass stem of Paavo Tynell's floor lamp are great examples of using the material sparingly for maximum results."

Unlike restrained mid-century furniture crafted from solid timber, fibreglass or plastic, rattan canes provide more visual intrigue while

→
A rattan console, seen in a ranch house in Montauk, New York.

↘
Rattan chairs on a Moroccan terrace—a perfect perch for textiles by Laith & Leila.

"As trade with the Far East increased in the eighteenth and nineteenth centuries, rattan was imported to Europe and made popular because of its strength and versatility."

↑
Atelier Vime's wicker and leather Bird Cage lantern is on the right and a 1950s rope table lamp from the archives on the left.

↓
Atelier Vime's The 20's vase, which errs on the side of the brand's more traditional-feeling pieces.

still adhering to a modern silhouette. "For me the great beauty of rattan is how sculptural designs made from it can be. It is not a material which is associated with any particular look or period," says Lytle.

Part of rattan's enduring quality is the versatility of its use. It plays nicely in a space and mixes well with other textures or materials. "Because the woven furniture tends to have a transparent quality, pieces that are more solid but have interesting colors or textures complement it really well, such as relaxed, generous linen sofas, tactile textiles in rich earthy tones, large ceramic urns and planters, and organic, sculptural furniture and lights," says Mamedovaite. "It's also beautiful to see rattan screens used as kitchen or wardrobe doors."

Roughly 20 years ago, China started developing an inexpensive synthetic material that mimicked rattan, and Indonesia in turn dramatically reduced the amount of raw material it was exporting. "It's a very emblematic story of world trade," Rauzy says.

While cheap, industrial furniture ultimately led to the decline of wicker furniture production in Europe, brands like Atelier Vime represent its backlash. The company was founded out of a frustration with the breakneck speed of furniture consumption. "We hope to question this mentality by showing this furniture as long-lasting, not something that you buy and use for one summer and then throw it away next summer because it's not fashionable anymore," Rauzy says.

Beyond sustainability, his argument for long-lasting furniture is that its value lies in its craft. It's the dignity of someone that spent days putting a piece together. It's thinking like this that paints a hopeful picture for rattan-crafted furniture—it's clear that wicker deserves a place of honor both in the home, and at the basketry festival in the village of Vallabrègues.

Woven Warmth

Humans have been weaving furniture from reeds for thousands of years—here are the designers who are doing it best today.

Bonacina is an Italian brand that has been bending rattan into shape since 1889. In the 1950s, the founder's son Vittorio recognized a new wave of design happening around him, and collaborated with several modern Italian designers like Agnoli Tito and Franco Albini on what are now iconic pieces that have been exhibited around the world. The family company is now in its fourth generation of Bonacina sons at the helm.

Based in New York with artisans around the world, fair trade production is at the heart of *The Citizenry* story. Their woven rattan pieces—among them chunky side tables and a handsome lounge chair—are made in close collaboration with makers in Indonesia, where the naturally growing rattan is locally sourced.

Mid-century pieces from the glory days of rattan furniture production are hard to find, and when they are, they do not come cheap. *1stdibs*, the online marketplace for vintage and antique furniture, has an extensive collection of rattan classics by Janine Abraham or Jacques Adnet that is easy to get lost in.

For more vintage woven furniture with a heavier-handed curation, try *Counter-Space*. The collection from the L.A.-based furniture seller is heavy on mid-century timber, caning, wicker, and bamboo, with the occasional woven classic like an armchair by Audoux-Minet.

In Barcelona, *Santa & Cole* refers to itself as an "editor" of well-designed products. Their portfolio spans urban street furniture like drinking fountains and bicycle racks, along with objects that work a little closer to home: pendent lighting or stackable wicker dining chairs by Ramón Bigas, designed in 1975.

A craftsman in the remote village of Kampung Naga in Indonesia who weaves decorative baskets out of rattan for New York-based brand, The Citizenry.

Rattan Salvador chairs by AOO, an update on the 1974 design by Miguel Milá.

Another Barcelona brand is _AOO_, which was founded in 2013 with a simple aim: to create functional, everyday furniture. What they have proven along the way, however, is that functional furniture can be beautiful, too. Among the beautiful pieces: a rattan chair designed by Miguel Milá in 1974, a classic they updated with colorful detailing.

Expormim was founded in Valencia in 1960 with the intention to export wicker products, a goal that nearly 60 years later, the company continues to achieve. In the 1970s, Expormim added rattan furniture to the repertoire, scaling up production to meet the weekly demands to line Mediterranean beaches with cane lounge chairs. Expormim has added new designers to the mix, like Jaime Hayon, while exploring the possibilities of woven furniture with their own internal research, development and innovation branch.

Agnes Studio is what happens when a Spanish designer reimagines furniture through the lens of PreColumbian and Mesoamerican history, with a dash of 1970s radicalism. Esoteric assumptions aside, these are chunky sculptural pieces with a dreamlike quality. For example, the Eclipse/Sol screen with mirror is a beautiful handwoven wicker design with sumptuous circles.

"As a reaction to the wave of minimalism and focus on machine-made perfection, there has been a return to craft and an appreciation for the process of making."

Turning a passion into a way of life has translated to an ambitious career for interior designer Serge Castella, who brings the vitality of the Mediterranean into his work.

Serge Castella

The idea that if you love something you set it free is not usually applied to home furnishings, unless they belong to Serge Castella. The French-born and Spain-based interior designer frequently acquires antiques for the home he shares with his partner in life and business, Jason Flinn, only to sell them to clients soon after. What he might love more than individual antiques is the thrill of finding new ones.

"Sometimes we have dinner at the house with clients and friends, and if people like something as much as I like it, I'm really pleased to sell it," he explains over the phone. "Because it gives us the possibility to find something else, which is what we like the most." With this last phrase, his voice changes and the glee is perceptible all the way from the hilltop in France where he's taking the call.

Castella has been trading antiques since 1990 and founded his interiors business in 2006. His projects mostly include private residences in southern Europe including Mediterranean beach shacks and Barcelona apartments alongside a colorful chalet in Chamonix and a jewelry store in Milan.

He seems to operate outside of the cycle of interior design trends, his spaces often defined instead by a curious collection of decorative objects and unexpected color and form. Flinn says he might pick up on something that isn't embraced by a larger public. "Five or 10 years later, it's everywhere. By then Serge is already onto other things." This approach has lauded him frequent press coverage in *Architectural Digest* magazines, where he was named one of *AD* France's top 100 decorators of the moment in 2019.

Castella and Flinn have lived in their home in the Empordà region of Catalonia—an hour from Barcelona and a 15-minute drive to the beach—for four years. The couple have been together for more than 30 years. What they've filled it with, Castella says, depends on the month. Archeology, 1950s modern, and contemporary all sit side by side, unified solely by Castella's eye. "I just assume it's working well together," he says. "It's not the same process that I'm going through with the customers, because my customers want to have the full idea before we begin. But when it's for me, I'm a lot more spontaneous."

"It was the center of the world for so long. The culture in the Mediterranean is fascinating all around. It's full of energy."

↑ →
Castella's Spanish home dates back to the 1970s. He and his partner, Jason Flinn, have worked on eight of their own personal residences together to date.

Serge Castella Interiors completes between eight and 10 projects per year, spanning mansions to seaside shacks and everything in between. The project that has Castella most excited at the moment is a large villa in the local region, where a very trusting client gave him total control of the house. Castella is painting everything white and furnishing it from top to bottom and the client will only see it for the first time when it's finished. "Usually clients like to look at everything with you. You do 75 percent of what you like. In this case it will be 100 percent," he says excited, adding, "and this is super."

Flinn, who grew up between Vermont and Hawaii, is a trained architect and oversees the

project's structural changes. The two have been collaborating on projects like this for almost as long as they've been together. Their office is a converted garage in the small town of Parlavà, where they work with three assistants. They opened this office two years ago, with a shop front selling antiques on street level.

Castella discovered his love of antiques while living in Paris, where he was studying fashion and spent his free time wandering the city's flea markets. "I realized that I was never going to fashion exhibitions, but I was always going to markets, to the galleries in St-Germain-des-Pres." he says.

In his early twenties, two things became clear. After stints with Parisian fashion houses Agnès B and Cacharel, he knew he wasn't interested in working in fashion. It was also clear that Castella, who grew up in the south of France, didn't want to be in Paris. "I wanted to live on the Mediterranean coast and I wanted to be free," he says. "I was ready to work a lot, but for myself." He moved down to Toulouse to open his first gallery specializing in Italian antiques and twentieth-century furniture.

His gallery began on a shoestring budget, where he was trying to sell pieces before paying for them. "The kind of things you do when you're trying to grow," he says. "It was fun!" Little by little the gallery grew, and eventually clients began asking him to decorate their homes with the pieces they bought from him, which led Castella to establish his practice 12 years ago.

Castella has remained on the Mediterranean coast ever since he moved back down to open his first gallery. In July and August, when the tourists descend in droves, the couple leave for America. Their summer home is a rustic Great Camp house in the quiet of New York's Adirondacks.

Castella and Flinn moved from France to Spain when they were looking for a property to breed horses. This is perhaps the most curious detail about Castella, that in addition to his career with interiors he and Flinn run a very ambitious program of breeding American Quarter Horses and Appaloosas. The horses no longer live on the same property as Castella and Flinn, having since been moved to near the Spanish border.

112

Serge Castella

Serge Castella

Castella does not limit the
interiors of his own home
with a stringent concept.
He mixes styles, periods, and
whatever catches his eye.

← ↑
Castella's home is constantly
changing. He will happily
sell his own antiques to
friends, only to be rewarded
with the thrill of finding
something to fill its place.
"The house we have now
corresponds to what we
need to feel good and what
we want to see when we
get up in the morning,"
says Castella's partner,
Jason Flinn.

The Mediterranean region has played a leading
role in Castella's life, not least of all as the backdrop to his work. "It was the center of the world
for so many cycles. The culture in the Mediterranean is fascinating all around—in the Arab
countries, in Greece, Italy, the south of France,
Spain. It's full of energy." In turn, he translates the
vitality of Mediterranean culture and context into
his interiors.

To do this he sets his sights way back, to the
region's ancient history. If his clients have the
budget for it, Castella will use classical archeological artifacts to reinforce a sense of place.
He combines these with local materials and the
modern necessities for comfortable, contemporary
living. "We try to give the Mediterranean feeling,"
he says. "But not a caricature of it. Just a feeling."

In the homes of his clients as well as his own,
Castella doesn't stick to a single period, style, or
theme. "If you do a home which is all Scandinavian, you're wrong, because we live in a world
that is very open. You can mix what people did
in the tenth century, which is as beautiful as what
people did in the 1950s," he says. "You can always
find a way to mix and it's what we try to do."

↗
"The outside of the house is a lot bigger than the inside, we have a lot of rooms to use six months a year," Castella says.

←
Castella spends as much time as he can perusing antiques. "It's a way of life," he says.

↑
The red hue of these homes comes from the red soil that was unearthed during their building and is complemented by local materials such as brick and wood.

→
Two bedrooms on the first floor of the 340 m² (3,660 ft²) apartment have intimate views of a pine tree forest.

Bringing the Outside Inside

These five weekend houses in Valle de Bravo, Mexico—two hours southwest of Mexico City—are quite literally rooted in the landscape. The homes are constructed from red soil that was unearthed during the excavation process, while laying the foundation—they are also made from local materials such as brick and wood. The 340 m² (3,660 ft²) apartments are identical, with a ground-floor kitchen and dining room, and two bedrooms above, peacefully surrounded by pine trees. Floor-to-ceiling glazing bathes each space in sunlight and cantilevered staircases outside give the houses a sculptural effect, while heat is sourced purely from the two fireplaces in each house. Designed by Héctor Barroso to include natural stone flooring and lightly textured brick walls, he explains that the houses were positioned to "generate a void, a central courtyard that grants views, silence, and intimacy." Building around existing trees whenever possible, some of the pine trees were cut and made into tables, benches, built-in cupboards, and kitchen cabinetry. It is this sense of place, the specificity of its materials and the notion of bringing the outside in, that defines this project and makes it stand out.

← ↑
Some of the pine trees
surrounding the houses were
felled and made into tables,
benches, built-in cupboards,
and kitchen cabinetry.

→
Each house is given a sculptural effect by the external
cantilevered staircases.

The Perfectionist's Paradise

←
Formerly a warehouse, this loft has been converted into a home with a terrace that looks out onto the Balearic landscape.

↑
The living room has chalk and mud-plastered stone walls, upon which art from Vroom & Varossieau gallery hangs, while the tan leather armchair is from The Modern Vintage—both of which are located in Amsterdam.

Formerly a workshop and storage unit in a rugged region of north Ibiza, interior architect Jurjen van Hulzen (owner of design studios Ibiza Interiors and The Nieuw) transformed a 100-year-old abandoned warehouse into a loftstyle home. It was when van Hulzen saw the $80\,m^2$ (861 ft^2) building and its unique location that the concept for the design was born. "It had been unused for many years, and was in very poor condition," he says. "Therefore, only the walls and parts of the roof could remain." Concrete floors complement the chalk and mud-plastered stone walls, and the structure has a wooden roof. Including the Sabina beams, all of the house's materials are local, except the powder-coated steel in the window frames, cupboard, and doors. The kitchen features an island with marble top from Eginstill; the elevated dining area shares the space with a built-in wooden bench and roof light. The walls are decorated with art from Vroom & Varossieau gallery in Amsterdam, with furniture, lighting, curtains, and carpets all from The Modern Vintage, also in Amsterdam.

↑ ↗
The 100-year-old building retains only its original walls and roof, while everything else was renewed, including the concrete floor.

→
Powder-coated steel is used for the window frames, which pick up the metalwork of the coffee table and sofa legs.

→|
Old olive trees surround the house.

Dysfunctional Modernism

↑
Surrounded by yucca trees and the Tepozteco Mountain range, the garden of this Santa Catarina home has outdoor sculptures that match the magnificence of the surrounding landscape.

→
The porch area includes objects gathered during Picault's travels, as well as leather seat cushions to soften the wood and metal-work chairs.

This country home, designed by Emmanuel Picault and his partner, architect Ludwig Godefroy, is a perfect blend of minimalist cool, brutalism, and Mexican warmth. Inspired by Le Corbusier, Marcel Breuer, Oscar Niemeyer, and Carlo Scarpa, as well as the ancient temples in Petra and Damascus, here modernism meets poetry. Surrounded by yucca trees and the Tepozteco Mountain range, the house is wider than it is tall, a pillared veranda overlooking a long, thin swimming pool (which becomes a lightbox at night) and an outdoor 1950s sculptures of a snake in a bright shade of orange. Its key materials are cement, whitewashed walls, and stone. The entrance door has Mayan symbols made by Spero Daltas in the 1960s. Woven straw chairs and bright pops of color via cushions, throws, and patterned rugs lend the living room an inviting energy, alongside a sculpture by Théo Mercier and a Bird armchair by Harry Bertoia. Elsewhere, a 1950s lamp by Eugenio Escudero illuminates a Moroccan Berber carpet and gold screen doors by Arturo Pani, a mix of registers that zing with energy.

|←
The entrance has gold
screens by Arturo Pani,
which complements a
Moroccan Berber carpet and
a 1950s lamp by Eugenio
Escudero.

← ↖
In the kitchen, raw stone
walls contrast with the met-
al cooking island, a variety
of glasses and delicate objects having been collected
from around the world.

↑
The living area combines art
and design pieces that nod
to modernism.

Next page:
Left: The long, thin
swimming pool becomes a
lightbox at night and also
features an orange 1950s
sculpture in the shape of a
Mexican snake.

Right: At the entrance are
Mayan symbols made by
Spero Daltas in the 1960s.

Rural Ibiza

At more than 400 years old, this Ibizan home is from another era, featuring original white textured stone walls and rustic wooden rafter ceilings. It was the traditional, rural Ibizan way of life that inspired the renovation of this Mediterranean home. Designer Pietro Cuevas wanted to strip the space and to expose its simplicity, leaving in features like the studded wooden doors and stone flooring. Comprised of two structures, one of which is a guesthouse, the main building has a joint kitchen-dining room decorated with vintage velvet green chairs and a chunky wooden table. The living area has a root wood armchair carved by Bali artisans. Elsewhere, the furniture mixes carved wooden chairs and wicker seats, woven matts, and low-lying sofas and beds. The light fixtures are particularly remarkable, huge bell-jar-shaped domes made of glass, which feel opulent though elegant. Outside, heavy vines grow across a doorway and a sun-worn turquoise table hints at the heat of Ibiza's bright blue skies.

← →
This 400-year-old home has original white textured stone walls and stone floors that have a cooling effect in the house. The shaded veranda, as well as roof rafters that prop up the ceiling, offer rustic touches.

↑
The living room features an armchair carved from root wood by Bali artisans, with a broad woven lampshade hanging above. The scene is rounded off by two small tables carved from a palm trunk.

←
Vines grow across the heavy, studded wooden doors, which are original.

→
The dining room's main feature is a rustic wooden table with green 1950s corduroy chairs and a bell-jar-shaped glass lamp from an old bar.

Can Xic

Mediterranean Modern

With a view of the Aegean Sea, this hotel on the island of Kos is based, like a traditional Greek settlement, around a central square, with numerous buildings made by Mastrominas Architecture. Each house takes the form of a modular cube shape with interior design by Berlin-based Lambs and Lions. OKU Kos is described as a place "where mid-century design meets hand-crafted Moroccan charm and natural textures." Straw sunshades are dotted around a swimming pool, which overlooks sand dunes and the beach. The buildings adjust to the weather conditions, with large sliding window frames that are secretly located in special niches; when the strong north meltemi wind blows, the beach-front window frames unfold. Inside, the rooms mix woven fabrics in neutral tones with chunky wooden furniture, wicker lamp-shades, and built-in Moroccan sofas. In each bathroom, huge mirrors reflect light around the minimalist space. Private terraces have CocoMat mattresses and rain showers making inside and outside equally livable.

←
Woven fabrics in neutral tones complement chunky wooden outdoor furniture.

↑
This hotel mixes mid-century design with Moroccan influences, from the wooden stools to the woven lampshades and wicker baskets.

→

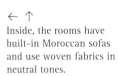
Inside, the rooms have
built-in Moroccan sofas
and use woven fabrics in
neutral tones.

→
The specific mode of built-
in Moroccan furniture
continues in the bathrooms,
where neutral-colored
surfaces are mounted with
chunky wooden shelves.

Bedroom fabrics range from
lightweight linen curtains
to thick-knit bedspreads,
as well as woven hessian
floor mats.

The bathrooms have brass
fixtures and large-scale mirrors reflecting light around
the room.

Next page:
Private terraces have natural
Coco-Mat mattresses and
rain showers, looking out
onto the Aegean Sea.

Celebrating the Mediterranean Aesthetic Through Details

↑
Objects used to decorate
Mediterranean-inspired
homes often include
ceramics that lend a crafted
feel inspired by antiquity.

Creating a sunny Mediterranean interior doesn't necessarily mean you need to live in the region. Here's how to evoke the right mood by combining modern artifacts with rustic and tactile home accessories.

Like wine, cheese, and other hallmarks of the Mediterranean region, its buildings often get better with age. That patinated texture of faded frescoes or sandy stuccoes blended with contemporary furniture creates an interior that is both rustic and modern. The problem is, we don't all live in the Med, and therefore our dwellings won't necessarily express that sun-drenched sense of place. Ezz Wilson is a stylist based in Portland, Oregon, a city known better for its un-Mediterranean characteristics, like cloudy skies and relatively young architecture. But this has never stood in her way when creating warm and welcoming spaces for herself and her clients.

It begins with a white wall. A simple, easy-to-achieve backdrop that is as practical as it is reminiscent of whitewashed walls in southern Europe. Next, the color palette. "Because I love white [walls] so much, I use little splotches of earth tones," says Wilson. She recommends warm colors to create a sundried quality: deep reds, burnt oranges, creams, and browns—all the shades of a Moroccan spice market. Rusty red cushions and wicker-woven accessories work especially well. "Because it's overcast and raining most of the year, it's pretty gloomy," she says. "So I realized

"There's a handmadeness to the Mediterranean approach to design."

↗
Crafted, tactile and light: jute and basketry is both functional and beautiful. The ones pictured here are by The Dharma Door, who work with female artisans in rural communities.

←
Baskets of Pampa woven by craftspeople in remote regions of Argentina. These are made from a native plant called the chaguar, which is similar to aloe vera.

I couldn't have a lot of cold colors in my room. I needed earthiness and I noticed that made a big difference psychologically, feeling warmer and not as chilled to the bone."

Dimitris Karampatakis, the co-director of Athens-based architecture and interior design practice K-Studio, takes it a step further. With a portfolio of hotels and restaurants dotted around the Mediterranean region, overcast skies pose less of a problem. In an atmosphere defined by the sun and sea, his work expresses a sense of leisure. "The Mediterranean is a place people go to relax," he says. "So things that speak to that, like a hammock or a lounge chair that's a little lower or deeper. Things that welcome you to recline and take it a bit slower."

A characteristic that underpins the region, says Karampatakis, is a sense of craft. "There's a handmade-ness to the Mediterranean approach to design," he says. "The decoration is out of necessity. Useful objects are crafted from real materials that carry a cultural heritage, such as stone, marble, clay. These are the usual suspects, and of course wicker, and linen, and unbleached linen fabrics."

Where Mediterranean architecture itself is missing, another trick is to echo its forms, which Wilson does with the Roman arch. "I love arched doorways," she says. "And I do have one that happens to be in my home, but I'd love to bring more of that in. I have a floor mirror that's arched out of textured wood, so that adds architectural interest to my room. You can add an arched mirror to your fireplace, mantle, or wall, or even paint an arch behind your bed or sofa."

Another benefit of white walls is that they offer a canvas for vignettes. "If you enjoy an object enough to have it on a shelf, it can also go on the wall," she says. "I also love religious items, prayer beads, icons, etc. I think adding a few wonky decorative items from thrift stores or craft fairs goes a long way." Woven bowls work especially well in a cluster, ditto straw hats. Part of the spontaneous joy of modern Mediterranean interiors is that anything can be decorative.

Atelier Studios' first collection, pictured throughout this spread, is inspired by the Italian relationship with food. The Australian brand's ceramics are crafted by artisans in southern Italy.

"Because the Mediterranean is such an eclectic mix of countries and cultures, and design approaches, I think eclectic is key if you want to have the Mediterranean feel," says Karampatakis. "You want to mix things from the north, south, east, and west of the Mediterranean and really create that amalgam of that big lake."

One of the best vignettes Wilson has ever styled was on her own living room wall. "I did it in five minutes because I had guests coming over and I had a bunch of crap lying around." To get rid of the clutter on the table, she took a hammer and nailed several plates, a rattan basket, a brass key, and a few postcards to the wall. The takeaway here isn't to try this at home—perhaps not all of us have such perfectly whimsical trinkets lying around—but to keep experimenting. "It's a puzzle, it really is," she says. For something a little more permanent, fringed wall hangings and rattan mirrors add a sense of craftedness to a space without the need to construct a composition.

Celebrating the Mediterranean Aesthetic Through Details

> "The decoration is out of necessity. Useful objects are crafted from materials that carry a cultural heritage, such as stone, marble, and clay."

"I think dried palm fronds really take me back to the Med," Wilson says. She recommends finding dried bunny grass from a craft store to lend a sun-faded feeling to a space, but she's also ordered palm fronds from California online. "It's such a simple way to add sculptural interest to a table or mantle," she continues. "Even if you don't have a Mediterranean plant in your eco system, you can always find something dried, brown, and dead in your backyard."

Dried plants are where another indicator of a modern Mediterranean sensibility comes in: the pottery in which to put it. After all, clay pots

and vessels reach back thousands of years in this region. "I love terracotta wine vessels; I think that's a really easy way to add a Mediterranean feel to a space," Wilson says. Renewed interest in ceramics means we are spoiled for choice when it comes to finding the right pieces.

Sophie Alda is a Bristol-based ceramicist and is inspired by pottery from the ancient world. One of her vases looks like a Grecian urn, but as if someone took the handles and stretched them into wide ears. "These vases are an exaggerated play on that ancient style," she says. Others have had a special glaze applied that gives one the sense of this being an archeological artifact. "It's a very satisfying texture, especially with that contrast of the clean bright blue and the straight line at the handle," she says. "It's like it has been pulled out of the sea."

To complement Wilson's palette of earth tones, Alda's ceramics mostly come in a vibrant pop of blue. "I'm absolutely in love with this cobalt blue," she says. The cobalt blue has a lovely matt finish—it recalls the color of roofs on the Greek Islands or the facade of the Yves Saint Laurent's house in the Garden Majorelle. Needless to say, it looks quite radiant against a white wall.

Ultimately, it's about finding the right contrast. Textured pieces like Alda's pottery, speckled ceramics, and handwoven details help create a lived-in quality in otherwise sparse interiors—"Just to keep things from looking too prim and proper," she says. For older buildings with more textured walls, contemporary pieces with clean lines play with the dynamics of old and new.

So how much is too much? Serge Castella, who is profiled on pages 110–119 of this book, carefully layers Mediterranean codes to keep things on the preferred line between inspired and pastiche. "It's just the way you dose it. If you put only the three or five important codes and temper them with modern things, it works." Otherwise, he continues, it turns into Provence 20 years ago. "It can just become an overdose of Provençal ceramics, Provençal fabric, Provençal everything! That is an extreme. When it's extreme, it disappears. Soft can stay for a long time."

Although this is entirely in the eye of the beholder, Wilson agrees that going big can be ephemeral. In the 1970s, if someone liked caning, for example, "They would take it and wallpaper their whole bathroom in cane and have a cane toilet and a cane sink, and it looks silly when you look at it now," she says. "I'm trying to create something a little more timeless that I won't laugh at down the road."

Wilson's home is in constant flux—her interiors change with different phases and her exploration of trends. "I keep core pieces that are modern and versatile that I won't get sick of in 10 years, like my sofa," she says, which is a cream-colored and flanked by a cane coffee table. The more expensive furniture pieces should feel permanent, modern, and versatile. "Then I can push it with other things and use the accessories to be a bit more experimental."

With so much noise in our daily lives, our homes increasingly play the role of calming respite. Ultimately, bringing the Med into your home is about considering what works for you. "I work in such a visual field, I crave not being overly stimulated when I'm home." As Wilson points out, the most important question to ask is: "What do you need when you come home?"

"Even if you don't have a Mediterranean plant in your eco system, you can always find something dried, brown, and dead in your backyard."

↑
A cozy corner in the home of Portland-based stylist Ezz Wilson. Dried foliage, basketry, and an earthy color palette are among her design staples.

→
Dried reed in its many forms creates a sun-drenched quality—even in not-so-sunny locations.

←
Classically inspired vases in a deep cobalt blue—a glaze devised by the ceramicist, Sophie Alda.

Shelfie Moment

When the walls are plastered and the furniture is in, all that's left are a few well-selected accessories to complete the picture.

The spirit of exploration thrives at _Couleur Locale_, a Belgian homewares boutique where you will find everything from Tunisian terracotta vases to Indonesian pendant lights to Ethiopian wooden bowls. If there is one thing demonstrated by the globe-trotting approach of the founders, it is that the home is the museum of the self: a space to be immersed in remnants of journeys past. For those less inclined to travel, they have a considerable selection in their online boutique.

The seeming simplicity of the sculpted clay plates, bowls, and vessels that Ana Kerin handcrafts for her brand _Kana London_ are the kind that make pottery look easy. Her expertly crafted range comes in an earthy palette of sand and mocha, with cheerful pops of color. Because so much of her work is born from experimentation with different mixtures of clay and glazes, each piece is a tactile experience—one that is beautiful to look at and pleasing to hold.

La Soufflerie is a Paris-based studio specializing in glassware hand-blown from recycled glass—a preservation of historic artistry, using traditional tools and processes. Their head pieces—little busts made from glass, plaster, and terracotta—feel like archeological artifacts. See also: beautiful carafes, jugs, and bottles blown from brown, clear, and green glass. As Karl Lagerfeld once said, "Nothing is more modern than antiquity."

Australians Melissa Jackson and Sven Geboers founded _Atelier Studios_ after traveling through Italy and meeting local ceramicists. Chance encounters turned into business partnerships: Atelier Studios works with a series of craftspeople in Sicily and Puglia on ceramics inspired by southern Europe. Their plates are especially charming, each painted with a different classically inspired face—no two are alike.

Portland-based interiors designer Ezz Wilson's style is a blend of modern and traditional, incorporating plenty of natural elements, texture and neutral layers.

Ben & Aja Blanc's mirrors and wall-hung sculptures are a sleek counterpoint to a rustic home. The American brand works with materials that give a timeworn impression, juxtaposed with sleek Mongolian horsehair.

A few of the oddities found on the _Kneeland Co_ online shop include classical Italian plaster casts of noses, Mexican Huichol beaded figurines, and 1960s puppets made in the Mexican state of Guerrero. Founder Joanna Williams has traveled extensively around the world on buying trips and has established her business as both a retail endeavor and as an interiors consultancy. The L.A.-based brand's sense of adventure comes naturally; Williams even named her business after her great-grandfather's 85-foot schooner.

Shannon Sheedy recognized that she could make a difference for craftspeople in places such as Nepal, India, and Indonesia simply by placing orders. Australia-based _The Dharma Door_ is part NGO, part home decorating business that champions makers by connecting them with customers around the world through her e-commerce boutique. Jute rugs woven in India, clay beaded garlands from Bangladesh, and decorative woven brooms (which are far more fun than the functional sort), are produced by a global network of craftspeople using traditional techniques and natural materials.

If there were to be a single characteristic that unifies everything by London-based ceramics brand _Milomade_, it would the sense of imagination that underpins the design of each piece. This is pottery that does not take itself too seriously. Speckled mugs have squiggly handles, vases form abstract faces with Roman noses, and pitchers have lumpy Michelin Man-like rolls at their base. And best of all? It all works.

Clay pinch-pots in the making by Kana London.

"Because the Mediterranean is such an eclectic mix of countries, cultures, and design approaches, eclectic is key."

Casa Mami | Pioneertown, California, USA | Design by Carlos Naude and Whitney Brown of Working Holiday Studio

Minimalist Desert Living

←
Casa Mami sits surrounded by the California desert.

↑
The living room's main feature is a Malm fireplace, reminiscent of the curvature of 1960s design.

In the heart of the Californian desert surrounded by an arid landscape of cactus and aloe plants, Casa Mimi is a Mediterranean sanctuary far from home. The designers and home owners, Carlos Naude and Whitney Brown, highlight how "a mix of cultures has definitely impacted the style." Converted from a one-bedroom house into a two-bedroom sanctuary, Naude and Brown took inspiration from legendary designers including Luis Barragán, Jacques Grange, and Terence Conran. With a clean minimalistic finish, the house is notable for its furniture—terrazzo tables, hessian rugs, and a vintage Malm fireplace for cold desert evenings—which sits within rooms flooded with sunlight that streams through huge windows and outswing La Cantina doors. Keeping the original structure and architecture, the entire color palette of the building's exterior was changed from terracotta orange to a sparkling white. The kitchen has Scandinavian touches, the black Smeg fridge contrasting with pale pink wood shelving, upon which beautiful earthenware is delicately stacked, ready for visitors to pour a cup of aromatic morning coffee and watch the sun rise.

→

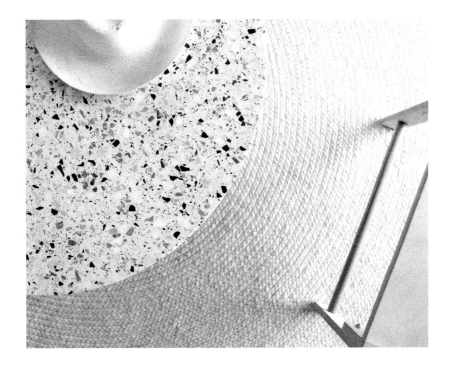

↑
Scandinavian touches define
the kitchen, with pale pink
shelving, a black Smeg
fridge, and a wide variety
of earthenware.

→|
The bedrooms have a clean
minimalist finish with a
geometric wall hanging,
wall-mounted side tables,
and an overhead fan.

| Hudson Valley Home | Croton-On-Hudson, New York, USA | Design by Roberta Thrun and GRT Architects |

Hudson Valley Modernism

↑ →
Built in 1962, this mid-century modern home has windows doubling as walls, long roof beams, and terra-cotta floor tiles throughout.

Designed by Roberta Thrun, who became one of the first female architects to graduate from Columbia University's architecture program in 1943, this mid-century-modern home was built in 1962 and sits on the east bank of the Hudson River. It uses rational design that connects to the natural world outside, huge windows doubling as walls to let in light and the landscape. To the south, the Tappan Zee bridge and Manhattan skyline are visible. Renovated by Tal Schori, Nathan Geller, and Rustam-Marc Mehta of GRT Architects, the trio were mindful of Thrun's original architectural vision from 60 years ago. The walls and windows are painted low-gloss black, with two roof beams sanded down, exposed, and waxed, revealing the warm grain. Original terra-cotta tiles comprise the flooring throughout, lending the house the warmth of the Mediterranean. The kitchen has a black workstation with industrial lighting above, while the black-and-white tiles in the bathroom create a sense of balanced and rational geometry, with a wink towards modernist aesthetics.

← ↑
Walls and windows are
painted a low-gloss black,
as are the kitchen's worksta-
tions so that the inside does
not distract from the nature
outside.

→
A sense of rational geometry
is conjured by the black-
and-white tiles in the
bathroom.

Inspiration from Outside

↑
The sunroom of this home has huge windows, flooding the space with light and revealing beautiful views. The soft linen Roman shades cover remote-control black-out shades beneath, which darken the room when needed.

A 1926 Spanish colonial house in Hollywood Dell, this 260 m² (2,800 ft²) home was designed by Los Angeles-based design firm Cuffhome. The plethora of windows in the home meant that color and texture were paramount. These include shades of oatmeal, cream, mustard yellow, terracotta, brick, and blush, with materials consisting of linen, velvet, and natural wood that blend with the backdrop of green plants. The home's original features range from stucco walls and architectural fireplaces to high ceilings and wood beams. In the living room a Casamidy coffee table contrasts with leather-wrapped Remnant stools by Cuffhome, alongside a mustard Swoon chair from Space Copenhagen. The guest bathroom has a Moroccan feel with white zellige tiles from Clé. Unique peach-colored spin art brightens up the children's room, while the dining room and sunroom are both multifunctional spaces used for eating, drinking, reading, homework, and play—the latter with a remote-control blackout shade under soft linen Roman shades.

↑
Tiles from Clé combine
with a handwoven rug and
woven baskets to lend the
bathroom a Moroccan feel.

↗ →
The numerous outdoor
spaces each create unique
opportunities to enjoy the
view from the house. Artist
Bradley Duncan created
outdoor containers for the
plants and built-in seating
and furnishings allowed the
outdoor areas to became like
a second dining room.

Rethinking the Ranch House

↑ →
The living room's wooden
roof beams were exposed
and painted white, while
the furniture mixes vintage
and original designs by
Studio Robert McKinley,
not least the round wooden
coffee table.

A ranch house originally built in 1978, this Montauk bungalow on Long
Island was fully renovated by designer Robert McKinley, who repainted the
space with a flat lime wash pigment and natural plaster finishes. "I drew
inspiration from Montauk's wild and salt-weathered coastline, and the casual
elegance of Europe's seaside towns where centuries-old cultures exude
rich color and pattern," says McKinley. The living room's drop ceiling was
removed and exposed, with wooden roof beams painted white, while another
sitting room is painted a deep red. The furniture is a mix of vintage and
original designs by Studio Robert McKinley, including a wooden coffee table.
The whitewashed bedrooms combine carved wooden furniture with textures
such as woven mats and long, white, summery curtains. The kitchen features
a 1970s-inspired breakfast nook alongside Reform cabinet fronts in charcoal
gray, while the bright bar stools add pops of color.

← ↑
Above the living area's stripped-back fireplace sit a variety of objects collected from around the world.

↗
A 1970s-inspired breakfast nook is a main feature of the kitchen, alongside Reform cabinet fronts in charcoal gray and brightly colored bar stools.

→
Carved wooden furniture, woven mats, and linen curtains decorate the bedrooms, as does a collection of straw hats.

McKinley Bungalow

Industrial Bohemia

"Cozy, with a bohemian touch and some multifunction elements," is how Susana Piquer of Colapso Studio describes this Barcelona apartment, which she designed. Indeed, the original tendril curves of the ceiling moldings have been perfectly preserved, and pick up on the patterned tiles that extend across the entire floorplan, both geometric and floral shapes rooting the 180 m^2 (1,938 ft^2) space.

↑
Tendril curves on ceiling moldings and patterned floor tiles are part of the original features of this studio home.

With four-meter-high walls, it is light and airy, large doors leading out onto a plant-filled balcony. The hall table, also by Colapso Studio, combines metalwork with wood, its minimalist industrialism mirrored by the low-rise table in the living room that was built using piles of house bricks. Lighting is a key focus, with the yellow vintage lamp in the main bedroom by Passeu Passeu and a Japanese-inspired floor lamp. Textures contrast in each room, not least the shaggy rug and Catalan stoneware in the living room. Such ceramic pieces from Mari Masot are presented upon raw wooden cabinets, with further accessories by Muji on the desk. All in all, it is this mix of registers, industrialism meets traditionalism, which defines the mood of this small Spanish residence.

↑
The living room mixes a
shaggy rug with Catalan
bricks, while large doors
open onto a lush balcony.

↗ →
Minimalist industrialism
defines the metalwork
furniture in the kitchen,
while the bedrooms have a
stripped-back elegance with
wooden bed frames and pale
gray linens.

Fading Beneath the Ibiza Sun

←
The blue-and-white palette
of this Ibiza home includes
distinctive floor tiles from
Mosaic del Sur with a wavy,
circular pattern, comple-
mented by towering cactus
plants.

↑
Rope, leather, stone, wicker,
and straw are used to create
a variety of textures through
the house, not least in the
living room, which includes
palm leaf stools, Ethiopian
coffee stands, and
Berber rugs.

This Ibiza vacation home was designed to feel faded and beachy, as if worn
down by sun and sand. Its blue-and-white color palette is complemented
by neutral and earthy textures. "I wanted a multitude of finishes from raw
brick to stone, rope, leather, wicker, and straw to create a base for the various
tones and patterns," says designer Hubert Zandberg. White walls and wooden
roof rafters offset the floor tiles, which range from herringbone to the iconic
geometric pattern of the pavement by Ipanema Beach in Brazil. The entrance
hall has a blue line painting by artist Tanya Ling, while the sitting room
mixes an Ethiopian coffee stand with a Berber rug, and a vintage Mexican
armchair. Locally sourced glazed ceramic tiles have a black pearlescent
finish, set against rustic wooden cabinets and seagrass pendant lights. The
bedrooms play with color and pattern and include a Once Milano yellow
bedspread and cushions from Fermoie. The guesthouse contrasts a La Maison
d'Alep glass pendant light with African gourd-shaped baskets, an antique
wood cabinet, brass mirrors, and vintage Spanish bamboo chairs.

←
The entrance hall features
a blue line painting by
Tanya Ling.

↗
Ceramic vases sit beneath
blue photograms of plants.

→

↖
In the guest bedroom,
custom cupboards were
manufactured by a local
cabinet maker.

←
The guest bathroom uses
a range of materials from
assorted blue glazed tiles
arranged in a herringbone
pattern, steel frame mirrors,
and glass wall lights to a
white pebble floor and ham-
mered brass basins.

↑ ↗
A bamboo pendant light
and seagrass frame mirror
are main features of the
main bedroom, with blue
scatter and seat cushions
using fabrics from Fermoie.

↑
Blue is the primary color in
the outdoor seating area,
which includes woven water
reed stools, sofa seat cushions using fabric from Jim
Thompson, and a rattan coffee table from Serena & Lily.

→
The courtyard dining area
has patterned Riviera Side
chairs from Serena & Lily.

Belgian designer Laurence Leenaert went from creating leather bags to designing products for the whole home— all she had to do was move to Morocco.

Laurence Leenaert

Marrakesh is an easy place to get lost. Shady paths wind deeper and deeper into the ancient medina, a labyrinth of hidden passageways where men leading donkeys or riding scooters seem to appear from nowhere. It's notorious for leaving people disorientated, especially newcomers. But for Belgian designer and Lrnce founder Laurence Leenaert, Marrakesh's medina provided a clear path to establish herself and her art.

After dropping out of her fashion masters at the Royal Academy of Fine Arts in Ghent, Leenaert founded LRNCE, a brand she intended would specialize in leather bags. But arriving in Morocco exposed Leenaert to a rich craft tradition. Four years since arriving, LRNCE has grown to include ceramics, textiles, sandals, mirrors, wall hangings, and kimono coats.

Leenaert connected with Morocco from the very beginning. She came on a holiday with her sister when she was 25, only to return four months later to camp in the desert and make leather satchels and travel bags out of old blankets.

"I was at a time in my life where I had no attachments in Belgium," she says. "There's so much freedom here. If you're creative, it's endless." A year later, in 2015, she decided to move to Marrakesh where she knew she could source high-quality leather and focus on making bags.

Morocco's ancient craft tradition sprawls many disciplines: pottery, glassblowing, weaving, tanneries—many of which are well represented in the medina by Berber artisans. In this respect, Morocco provided fertile ground for experimentation and Leenaert was in the right mindset for it. "When I moved here, I promised myself I would be very open to try whatever I want, and that I wouldn't put myself in a box." Eventually an artisan asked if she would like to make some sandals. "And I was like, 'Why not!'"

When you know one good artisan, it's only a short time before you meet another and another, the designer explains. And in meeting new artisans, Leenaert encountered new disciplines. One family invited her over for couscous on a Friday night and asked if she'd like to paint some pottery.

> "I had no attachments in Belgium. There's so much freedom here. If you're creative, it's endless."

One thing led to another, and now LRNCE sells ceramic vases, cups, and plates made out of clay from Fes and painted white with mustard, blue, and rusty red scrawls.

Her pieces reflect the sun-drenched environment that surrounds her, with colors derived from the dusty landscapes and clay buildings. Motifs such as the Eye of Fatima are painted on ceramics based on her observation of these motifs drawn on the doors of people's homes. Her loosely arranged compositions and the playful movement of her paint brush has created a body of work that vibrates with joy.

Although LRNCE's collection is entirely Moroccan-made using locally sourced materials, the brand doesn't try to reinvent traditional design. Instead, it's a contemporary interpretation that blends the local context with her western background. This didn't always go seamlessly. There was one instance where Leenaert's spontaneous painting caused a stir with a ceramicist. "They were like, 'Oh my god, you're ruining everything!' They didn't understand why they spent so much time making such a nice vase and in two minutes I made a mess of it."

But where she didn't always find encouragement from the locals, she found it on Instagram. When she posted a photo of her ceramics, the enthusiastic response was enough to show she was onto something. "This is how it all started actually, on Instagram," she says. "Otherwise no one would know what I was doing here."

The Marwaa two-part pouf: handwoven in Marrakesh by local craftspeople with irreverent designs by Laurence Leenaert.

The boutique adjacent to Leenaert's studio in Sidi Ghanem, Marrakesh. She keeps the walls white to celebrate the colorful stock.

Laurence Leenaert

Laurence Leenaert

"As confusing as it can be at first, I'm really happy I lived there because I think you have to live in the medina to get it."

←
The color palette is derived from the Moroccan surroundings, free-flowing forms are applied across textiles, ceramics, art, and apparel.

↗
Although originally more interested in fashion, Leenaert began experimenting with decor. The enthusiastic response she found on Instagram was an impetus to pursue it further.

↑
Along with homewares, LRNCE produces leather bags, sandals, and kimono-style garments.

Laurence Leenaert

Leenaert spent two years in the medina learning Moroccan craft and defining her own. "I'm really happy I lived there because I think you have to live in the medina to get it. As confusing as it can be at first, it doesn't take long before you know everyone and everyone knows what you're up to."

It took some time, but she's now found a trusted group of 35 artisans, each in their own atelier, who look after production. It's a true collaboration, she says, one that wouldn't work if she lived remotely. "You really need to be there every day and talk to them. This is how they appreciate what you're doing."

She's since moved into a 200-yearold adobe house just outside the medina, with a studio and shop in the industrial neighbourhood of Sidi Ghanem. The large space is lined with windows and full of plants, the walls intentionally kept white to draw attention to the products. Her mornings are spent here with her team of nine designing new pieces and producing samples. In the afternoon when the boutique opens, she goes out to meet with the artisans.

Life in Morocco may be a departure from the Belgian city Leenaert grew up in, but perhaps therein lies why the response to her work has been so positive. It combines a familiar European approach but bathes it in the color and light of the warm, southern climate.

Understanding the simplicity of the Berber way of life was a strong impetus to move to Morocco in the first place. Leenaert has always been interested in African tribes and how they express their identities. Whenever possible, she'll leave the city to go back to the Berber communities in the desert and Atlas Mountains to escape the traffic-choked city and observe how the tribes live, how they dress, and how they paint their homes.

"It makes you realize we have so much stuff in our houses in Europe," she says. "It helped me leave my life in Belgium behind." A Berber family might live and sleep all together in one room lined with clay walls and filled with not much more than blankets on the floor and a small table. Two items are key, however: an oven for baking daily bread and a television. "Here quality of life is about being healthy and surrounded by family. Things don't have to be fancy for people to be happy," she says. "I think the state of mind is so different here."

←
Leenaert spends her mornings working from her studio, before heading out in the afternoons to meet with the artisans.

↑
Framed works are made from naturally dyed wool, embroidered by hand onto an off-white wool canvas.

↖
All ceramics are painted in Marrakesh using clay sourced in Fez.

←
Cheerful scrawls on hand-made pottery. "I make a lot of mistakes, like paint dripping, but this is what makes it beautiful."

↑ →
Details from the LRNCE studio. "It's very open, everyone sees each other," she says. "I feel the artisan vibe, but still it's modern."

Medina Minimalism

Set within the bustling streets of Marrakesh's medina, Riad 42 is a white-washed minimalist house. Designers Sarah and Grégoire Rasson say they instantly "fell under the charm" of the place. Its original scalloped wooden windows, doorways, and intricate balcony were maintained and integrated into the riad's essentialist style. Dark gray, neutral beige, and white tones contrast with cactus gardens and banana trees potted in huge ceramic vases. A shallow marble fountain is set within a polished tadelakt plaster patio, the bhou alcove seating set deep and lined with white linen. The five bedrooms have woven textiles and hand-loomed wool blankets—many of which were made by the Berber communities in the nearby Atlas Mountains—as well as ensuite bathrooms with tadelakt floors, molded sinks, simple brass fittings, and open showers. The high ceilings leave room for elaborate metalwork and woven straw light shades hanging above four-poster beds. Low-slung sofas, Malian mats, and an exposed brick fireplace make the riad warm in the winter, while a sail-like tent shades the roof terrace in the summer.

← →
This Marrakesh riad's essentialist style includes original features such as scalloped wooden windows, doorways, and intricately patterned balconies.

Previous page:
Left: Woven mats from Mali
create cozy seating areas.

Right: The bedrooms have
wooden four-poster beds,
hand-loomed wool blankets,
and rugs by Morocco's
Berber communities.

↑
A woven lampshade against
a raw stonewall.

↗
The rooftop has a long
rectory-like table for eating,
as well as sail-like tents beneath which to take shade.

→|
Low-slung sofas, metalwork
lamps, and carved African
sculptures adorn the courtyard's seating areas.

Casa No Tempo | Alentejo, Portugal | Design by Manuel Aires Mateus
and Silent Living

Traversing Time

This Portuguese home has traversed generations, passing from grandfather to grandchildren. The family explaining, "It was our granddad's will that we look after the home for the next generation." The house is an heirloom— albeit one with a contemporary edge. Set within a property of 1,000 acres, the surrounding landscape is dotted with cork trees, its pastures and wild fields animated by flowing streams, babbling brooks, two dams, and five ponds—plus a 400 m² (4,300 ft²) swimming pool. The house is elegantly geometric, its wide structure and pointed roof intersected by a grand arched doorway. Designed by Manuel Aires Mateus, inside, the floors throughout

↑
The house has 1,000 acres of land, which includes cork trees, pastures, wild fields, streams, dams, brooks, and ponds.

→
The outdoor area beneath a grand arch features this large wooden table and benches, from which the vast landscape expands.

are paved with local clay blocks, which are heated in winter for warmth. A fully equipped kitchen is open to the vast dining room, which is furnished with pristine white sofas that complement the brightness of the beautiful corner fireplace. The four bedrooms have walk-in showers with handmade tiles, illuminated by Davide Groppi lights and beds, in which you could sleep forever, by Living Divani.

↑
Floors are paved with local clay blocks, which are heated in cold winter months.

→
The lounge is pure white, with the sofas blending into walls and a huge window revealing the wildflower fields outside.

→|
The lounge opens into the kitchen-diner, which has a solid wooden table and minimalist hanging lights.

← ↑
Low-lying white sofas are the best vantage point from which to curl up by the corner fireplace, while stacks of books give a homey feel.

→
When João and Andreia Rodrigues's grandfather left them the house, they renovated the building which is set in an idyllic countryside location.

| Casa No Tempo

Paros's Timeless Simplicity

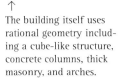

The building itself uses
rational geometry includ-
ing a cube-like structure,
concrete columns, thick
masonry, and arches.

↗ →

Natural materials merge
with a soothing color palette
and an eclectic collection
of vintage and modern
furniture, from Greek design
pieces to ceramics sourced
in North Africa.

Parilio hotel is on the Greek Island of Paros, where people move to the slow
rhythm of Cycladic life. Owners Kalia and Antonis Eliopoulos employed
Athens-based Interior Design Laboratorium for the fourth time to create a
hotel. Structurally, the 33-suite hotel looks like a cubist form that is defined
by its geometry, arches, concrete columns, and thick masonry—the architects
were influenced by the island's own distinctive architecture and serenity.
The hotel has a neutral color palette of whites that are complemented by
the deep Mediterranean earth tones featured on woven fabrics including the
bedspreads. The furniture is a mix of vintage and modern pieces, both by
contemporary Greek and European designers, alongside ceramics from
North Africa. The vast swimming pool looks onto the wild beauty of
Paros's pastoral landscape, and the idyll is just minutes from the beautiful
Kolimpithres Beach.

Algarve Sanctuary

Set in the Ria Formosa Natural Park in southern Portugal's Algarve region, this voluminous 1940s building sits by a salty lagoon. Converted from a family house into a hotel by architects Par Plataforma de Arquitectura, and using materials from clay tiles, red limestone, and cork insulation to brass hardware the project's designers were The Home Project, also know as Álbio Nascimento and Kathi Stertzig. They were guided by the owner's reference to their "grandfather's passion for self-made artistic interventions [hand-made objects] and his collection of vernacular furniture." A series of exterior stairways lead up to a flat roof; beneath this, the interior's brick ceilings arch and lend each room an altar-like calm. A built-in fireplace brings warmth through the winter months. The furniture is from both local designers and family heritage, with solid wood furnishings made by Lacecal. Terracotta pots, stripped ceramics, and wall-mounted plates are gathered throughout, this collection of clay contrasting with the solidity of wood and brickwork.

←
Decorative terracotta pots
and vases are gathered
throughout this house, not
least on this stairway, which
is laid with regional
clay tiles.

↑
This 1940s-era building has
dramatic external staircases and sits next to a salty
lagoon and fruit trees.

→

← ↓
The built-in fireplace is decorated with handmade objects and hanging cloves of garlic, while stripped ceramics and wall-mounted plates are gathered throughout the building.

→
Rooms have arched brick ceilings for an altar-like quality.

↘
The furniture throughout is made with wood from both Canadian west coast forests and Germany's Black Forest, from red cedar to Douglas fir trees.

Next page:
Nestled within the Algarve's Ria Formosa Natural Park, this building is surrounded by nature and mixes white walls with clay floors.

Casa Modesta

Casa Modesta

Joie de vivre is paramount for this Athens-based practice, which specializes in hotels and restaurants in coastal sunny locales.

K-Studio

Dimitris Karampatakis will be the first to tell you that the Greeks know how to have a good time. "There's a common understanding that as Greeks, we have a warm heart and a social culture," he says. "That comes from the warmer climate, the proximity to the sea, and the culture of tourism." After all, this is a country that invented the term "xenia," an ancient concept of hospitality, and Dionysus, the ancient god of wine.

This joie de vivre was one of the deciding factors that steered Karampatakis Studio, the architecture practice he established with his brother Konstantinos in 2002 (renamed K-Studio in 2010), from working in residential design to a focus on hospitality. The result is a portfolio of beachfront, pool-side hotels and restaurants that blend traditional with contemporary, each beckoning their guests to kick back and enjoy the Mediterranean breeze.

"We actively steered the studio into leisure architecture because we felt that, in a way, Greeks are leisure experts," Karampatakis says from his studio in Athens, where he and his brother run a team of 52 architects and interior designers.

Although K-Studio's portfolio is concentrated on the Greek Islands—including the Casa Cook Chania hotel in Crete, Vora villas in Santorini, as well as Scorpios beach club, Branco hotel, and Alemagou restaurant, all in Mykonos—the focus on hospitality has helped them attract international commissions. K-Studio has completed projects in America, the U.K., Turkey, and Spain.

Their style of their architecture is location dependent. Barbouni, for instance, is a beach restaurant in the Peloponnese region of the Greek mainland that sits amid the dunes like a giant modern sandcastle. It was completed in 2011, but had a brush with fame seven years later when a post of the restaurant's ceiling went viral.

This attention isn't unfounded. The ceiling is crafted from hundreds of strips of fabric cut in a wave formation to mimic the sea, moving psychedelically when animated by the wind. "We were really interested in making a place that responded to the dynamic nature of its surroundings," Karampatakis says. In this windswept corner of the earth, the building is always moving.

Barbouni's timber structure is coated in a sandy render selected to match the tone of the beach, and sits on an elevated platform in order to share the building's footprint with the local sea turtles. "I'm very happy to say the turtles have laid eggs right under the structure, which means they've welcomed it, hopefully," he says.

Karampatakis and his brother have always been close to architecture. "Our father is an architect and a developer, so I think he brainwashed both of us. We didn't stand a chance," he laughs. They grew up visiting their father's construction sites and both went on to study at The Bartlett School of Architecture in London.

It was while they were working at the practice of the Stirling Prize-winning Will Alsop—with no intention of returning to Athens—that the brothers received their first architectural commission at home from a friend looking to redo his house. That became the turning point for the duo to establish their own practice, which they did in 2002 when Karampatakis was 23. "We both realized that it would be a big risk to take, but we were willing to do it together," he says.

Another pivotal point for the studio came later in 2017 with a residence in Milos. "We very quickly saw that it was a very good opportunity to learn more about traditional architecture by renovating an existing structure from the 1800s," he says. With its deep white walls, stone floors, and small windows, the building falls within the lineage of the traditional architecture of the Cycladic Islands—a cluster of Greek Islands most commonly exemplified by picture postcard images of Santorini.

"It's fantastic to go to a place which has a lot of history, from materiality to construction techniques, and to try and bring that in as a palette and yet not feel bound by it," Karampatakis says. Bridging the house's historic atmosphere with the needs of modern life was the challenge. The home is filled with terracotta light fixtures, woven furniture, and linen textiles, all of which were selected by K-Studio. "Even the towels," adds Karampatakis. The window shutters are a cheerful shade of Greek Island blue.

Karampatakis and his brother have also always been close to the Greek Islands, especially Mykonos, where they spent their childhood summers. Since then, Mykonos has grown and grown. It's increasingly popular with tourists from

"We actively steered the studio into leisure architecture because we felt that, in a way, Greeks are leisure experts."

← ↑
This nineteenth-century house on the Greek Island of Milos was restored from the ground up. The client was a London-based family. The town's narrow streets meant the building materials had to be transported by hand from the nearest road.

around the world, but therein lies the opportunity for K-Studio. Hospitality projects—like Alemagou, a beachfront restaurant with a ceiling made from dried grass, or Scorpios, a beach club with blocky wooden furniture and hammocks in the lobby—have given the brothers a reason to return.

One of those projects is Branco, a hotel marked by its sequence of indoor and outdoor spaces. Each room has a private courtyard, a place to de-sand and de-salt with an alfresco shower after a day at the beach. It's in thoughtful details like this that you can trace the connection to the brothers' childhood summers in Mykonos.

"Wherever we go, we try to understand the place deeply. A familiarity with place became such a part of our design process, and this takes a lot of research," he says. "Wherever we go, we try to be that little kid."

↑
Branco hotel in Mykonos was heavily influenced by traditional Mykonian architecture: whitewashed walls, solid timber frames, and screed floors.

→
A series of courtyards accompany each room, providing a space to de-sand before arriving indoors.

↑
The ceiling of beach-side
restaurant Barbouni moves
with the wind, designed
to echo the movement of
the sea. "It felt wrong that
we make something that is
totally static," says architect
Dimitris Karampatakis.

→
The restaurant, which blends
in with the color of the
sand, was nominated for
the prestigious Mies van der
Rohe award in 2013.

 Furniture at Dexamenes
Seaside Hotel was selected
to contrast with the stark
industrial shell, to create
an environment that feels
contemporary and cozy.

→

Dexamenes is housed in a
disused wine factory that
has been largely untouched
since the 1920s.

"It's fantastic to go to a place that has a lot of history, from materiality to construction techniques, and bring that in as a palette, yet not feel bound by it."

↑
The hotel rooms are in the former wine storage rooms, which over time have developed a beautiful patina on the concrete walls.

| Casa Kastellorizo | Kastellorizo Island, Greece | Design by Architetti Artigiani Anonimi |

Sail Away

A typical Dodecanese home from the late-nineteenth century, this house on the Greek Island of Kastellorizo was converted by architect Annarita Aversa and features exposed brick walls and wood-panel ceilings. The adage of architect Peter Zumthor was Aversa's guiding principle during the redesign: "The old is old, don't restore; preserve or design." A color palette of Mediterranean turquoise blue runs throughout the house, from the window frames and doorways to the sofa, stairs, kitchen cabinets, cupboards, and even the bed upstairs. The upper floor and floating staircase are both connected to the roof by blue poles. Exposed brass pipes for the electrical systems run throughout the house and their geometric lines complement the rustic nature of the building. The new ground flooring is made of blue glass, suggesting the deep blue sea that is just meters away. With the furniture mainly made using straw and wood, this is a traditional Greek tavern with a fresh, modernist edge, combining old and new.

↖ This typical Dodecanese home from the late-nine-teenth century is painted in varying shades of blue, which reflect the sea that laps at its doorway.

↑ A moving staircase is connected to the roof by blue poles.

→

←
The exposed brick walls
are complemented by the
flooring, which is made of
slightly reflective blue glass
made in Italy.

↑
From the window frames
and doorways to the sofa,
kitchen cabinets, and
cupboards, all are rendered
in varying intensities of
turquoise blue.

← ↑
An exposed electrical system runs along the restored stone walls through brass pipes that are visible upstairs in both bedroom and bathroom, the bed having been made by design studio Architetti Artigiani Anonimi.

The Earth House

Gorgeous colors pop in every room of this house, from the fluorescent pink chairs of the dining room to the green ceramics in the kitchen. Architectural features include bamboo lattice ceilings and earthenware tiles on the wall. The brightly woven fabrics of each space are typical of Morocco, with pillows and throws made by local craftspeople.

↑
A bamboo lattice ceiling shades the botanical garden of this Moroccan home.

→
The bedroom features contrasting textures, from the tiles on the wall and the woven fabric cushions, bedspread, and basket, to the Malian mat and carved wooden tables.

It was quite by chance that landscape architects and interior designers Arnaud Maurières and Eric Ossart stopped in Taroudant in the 1990s. They settled there in 2003 to build this earth house surrounded by a botanical garden, which they describe as synthesizing the travel and research that they did over a period of 20 years. Outside, the terrace doubles as a plant nursery, with a combination of cacti and arid landscape plants. Inside, the living room required major renovations to make way for the arches, the denim-upholstered benches and carpets woven by the nomadic desert tribe Aït Khebbach. Terracotta floor tiles run throughout and in the kitchen they are combined with pale blue tiles—together they recall the warmth of the Mediterranean, land, and sea together.

← ↗ →
The dining chairs in the
kitchen have been painted
fluorescent pink, while
ceramic plates with typical
Moroccan designs are
mounted on the wall and
green ceramics are stacked
upon the shelves.

↑
A single bedroom uses
elaborately patterned and
colored fabrics, with woven
lampshades overhead.

←
The living room's denim-upholstered benches are scattered with bright cushions and offset with carpets woven by the nomadic Aït Khebbach desert tribe.

|←
The ceilings are typical of Moroccan design, featuring tightly packed sticks supported by larger wooden beams.

→

→
The outdoor dining area
includes a terrace with
chunky wooden stools and
a rustic table alongside cacti
and arid landscape plants,
effectively doubling as a
plant nursery.

Inspiration from California

↑
The living room includes
a wood-burning stove that
keeps the space warm in the
winter months. With a mix
of wood and terracotta tile
flooring, the room's textures
also include velvet seating
and a woven side table.

Riverside House, a guesthouse in Normandy, mixes a California costal lodge
vibe with a sense of nineteenth-century France. "My inspiration for this
house are my memories as a kid, when I would long to escape the city," says
American owner and designer Jordan Feilders, who designed the house
together with his French wife, Tatiana Dupond. "I grew up fishing in north-
ern California on trips with my grandfather and camping on a remote lake
in Canada." Filled with furniture from the nineteenth century, including the
armoire, mirrors, table, and chairs, interspersed are a selection of Italian modern furnishings, including the brown velvet sofa. The living room includes
a woodburning stove and a side table and coffee table made using the palest
wood matched by a natural woven rug. Feilders renovated the space to include
solid oak wooden shelving and pine cabinets behind the beds on the second floor. The art is sourced from flea markets, family members, and artists
including Caroline Denervaud.

↑ →|
Rustic wooden beams in the
bedroom support the roof,
their chunky texture echoed
in these solid wood bedside
tables.

↗
The kitchen combines solid
cement counter tops that
were made in Paris with a
brass splash back panel that
runs along the walls, made
with brass sourced from
Tartaix in Paris.

→
The terrazo stone used in the
bathrooms was sourced in
Italy and lines the walls behind a bespoke ceramic sink.

A Beachy Chateau

Surrounded by vineyards in the Médoc region of southern France, this home designed by Olivia Thébaut is only 20 minutes from the Atlantic Ocean. Hanging in the garden's hammock, this feels like beachside living fused with the mood of a lowkey traditional French chateau. Timeworn walls are offset by ceiling rafters that are coated with a lick of white paint. Straw mats overlay original tiled floors, a harlequin pattern of terracotta and cream. Pampas grass is arranged in clear glass jars and, likewise, wild flowers picked from nearby fields are dotted throughout in ceramic pots. The furnishings are vintage, from the sideboards and the low-lying wooden sofas covered with linen cushions, to the bamboo chairs. Thébaut is both a stylist and photographer. "My interest in photography started when I was working as an art director," she says, which is probably why her immaculately styled house photographs quite so beautifully. The kitchen is all white and wood, with details including the large straw lampshade and varied terracotta cups—drink up the elegance.

← →
The original flooring has a harlequin pattern, while the timeworn walls are elegantly mottled with pastel tones.

Home of Olivia Thébaut

↑
A bamboo chair sits next to a low-lying wooden sofa, both covered with linen cushions.

←
Wild flowers sit next to a woven basket, art history books, and a ceramic vase.

→

Home of Olivia Thébaut

| ←
The whitewashed kitchen has original roof rafters and uses a variety of wooden furniture, from the sideboard to the table and chairs, finished off witha large, straw lampshade overhead.

←
The kitchen's plates, jugs and glasses range from ceramic to terracotta and glass.

Handmade Heaven

 The kitchen is solid wood and handpainted white, and features a handmade terrazzo countertop and an elegant but efficient shelving system.

 Bleached pine floors and slanted windows and ceilings define the top-floor apartment in this townhouse, with the living area featuring a sofa by Paola Navone for Gervasoni.

Home of Caroline Feiffer

↖ ↗ →
Custom-built furniture,
closets, shelving, and cabinets were made by Feiffer's
woodworker husband,
Stefan, lending the space
a consistent aesthetic.

Situated on the top floor of a 1737 Copenhagen townhouse by Frederiks-
holms Kanal, this bright apartment has plenty of windows and tall slanted
ceilings. Designer and resident Caroline Feiffer decided to replace the floors
with bleached pine and remodel the kitchen, which now has a handmade
terrazzo countertop. The closets, shelving, and cabinets were all custom-built
by Feiffer's husband, Stefan. The living area features a sofa by Paola Navone
for Gervasoni, as well as a bench handmade from Douglas fir wood and lacquered a reddish-brown shade. The lamp is a Viennese piece from the 1980s
made with woven raffia. In the bedroom, the whitewashed space has crisp
linens on the bed, while the bedside lamp is a stoneware design by Per and
Annelise Linnemann-Schmidt for Palshus with a cloth shade by Christopher
Farr. The entire home is in bright shades of cream and white, while an atelier
space above the entrance hall and kitchen functions as a small study with
a 1950s Carimate chair by Vico Magistretti for Cassina.

White walls, vaulted ceilings, stone floors—
Andrew Trotter creates contemporary spaces
with rustic Italian charm.

Andrew Trotter

Andrew Trotter spent most of his childhood drawing modern architecture. Although he'd designed more than 200 houses by the age of 18, he says, it wasn't until the age of 44 that he actually built one.

Masseria Moroseta, a whitewashed Mediterranean farmhouse nestled comfortably among Puglia's blue skies and olive groves, is the designer's first completed architectural feat. Judging by the success of the six-room guesthouse, heavily Instagrammed and fully booked, it certainly won't be his last.

With thick walls and arched ceilings, rustic textiles and ceramic details, and a cacti garden arranged in sparse precision, the building's rustic and minimal sensibility translated Trotter's signature style into the built form itself, which until then had been established solely across art direction and interior design.

Born in the north of England, educated in Australia, and now living in Barcelona, Trotter made a name for himself when he founded Openhouse in Barcelona. The business began as a high-end design boutique and slowly evolved into a gallery in his own home, where he and his

collaborator and flatmate, Mari Luz Vidal, hosted exhibitions, talks, and supper clubs. In three years, more than 4,000 people walked through the door. Now Openhouse has transformed into a magazine, one that picks up on the theme of opening up one's home. In its pages, creatives around the world have opened their doors to readers in 11 issues and counting.

At Masseria Moroseta, this spirit of openness also plays a role. Founder Carlo Lanzini wanted to create a home for himself as well as a guesthouse that would provide visitors with a communal experience in the Italian countryside. He originally enlisted Trotter to help him find an old house to do up.

"We went to Puglia a few times, but we couldn't find the right old building in the right place," says Trotter from his small office in Barcelona. When Lanzini found the perfect piece of land overlooking the sea, he asked Trotter to help him find an architect, and he quickly volunteered to do it himself.

"When I was a kid I always wanted to be an architect, but when I moved to Australia it was

> "I started to really look and realized that the old buildings, especially in Ostuni, were very minimal. Vaulted ceilings, white walls, stone floors and nothing much else."

↑
Villa Castelluccio is a three-bed and three-bathroom home in the Puglia countryside. The interior, which was renovated three decades prior, needed renovating to reduce the 1980s feel in favor of something a little more timeless.

→
The original limestone tiles were retained, but polished to reduce their shine.

difficult to get into architecture there, so I did interior design instead," he says. "It was really a dream for me to be able to explore and learn how you build a house."

It takes a degree of trust for a first-time hotelier to hand the reins to an untrained architect, no less after Trotter's first design was rejected by the local council for being too modern. But this, it turned out, was a good thing. "I started to really look and realized that the old buildings, especially in Ostuni, were very minimal. Vaulted ceilings, white walls, stone floors, and nothing much else."

Trotter completed Masseria Moroseta with the help of a local technical architect, who realized his design vision into structural reality. Trotter, who speaks just enough Italian to work with local builders, oversaw the construction and the interiors implementation.

Historic houses with an unintentionally modern sensibility informed Masseria Moroseta's design, making it a modern space that sits comfortably with its historic neighbors. "The biggest compliment I get is when people ask, 'Which part is old?' or 'How old was the building when you found it?'" Trotter says. "I reply, 'No, it's all new.'"

It's an easy mistake to make. The building follows the tradition of the local fortified farmhouses, and is built using limestone sourced in the immediate region. Trotter also designed every nook and cranny to be photographable, which has served him well when it comes to publicity. He's now busily working on 11 architecture commissions, each of which came via people who have either stayed at Masseria Moroseta or seen the space online.

One of these new commissions is Villa Castelluccio. The owner sold her home in Ibiza, after staying at Moroseta, in order to work with Trotter on rebuilding a Puglia farmhouse that was built in the 1920s and renovated in the 1980s. "I shouldn't even say we modernized it," he says.

Andrew Trotter

← Trotter updated the landscape surrounding Villa Castelluccio. "I don't like if everything is manicured. I prefer farmland that's been tweaked a little bit," he says.

↙ Villa Cardo, also located in Puglia, was completed in the spring of 2019. The cacti overlook a rose-colored pool.

↓ Like Moroseta, the three-bedroom Villa Cardo was designed in keeping with the local architectural vernacular.

→ The kitchen at Villa Castelluccio was entirely redone. The bespoke kitchen tops are made from concrete.

Andrew Trotter

← ↑
Besides its purpose as a
guesthouse, Moroseta is
also a functioning olive oil
farm. The product is nutty
in flavor, Trotter says, and is
"Good with just about anything." Masseria Moroseta
was Trotter's first completed
architectural commission.
The design echoes the white
walls and arched ceilings
of traditional architecture
in the region.

→
A core tenet of the Moroseta
experience is a sense of
togetherness. Communal
spaces like this one show
how the design supports
that intent.

Andrew Trotter

| Andrew Trotter

↖
Numeroventi brings
together artist residencies,
apartments and an exhibi-
tion space under one roof
in a sixteenth-century
Florentine palazzo.

↑
Numeroventi's
Apartment #2 is a contem-
porary counterpoint to the
more historic-feeling parts
of the villa, where original
frescoes have been retained.

"I think we made it feel older." Like Moroseta, its deep white walls are punctuated with rustic details like textiles and local ceramics. "I was very lucky with Villa Castelluccio that the owner, Jane, has a wonderful eye. Together we went to the markets searching for special finds."

Numeroventi is another project in Italy that came to Trotter via a former guest—this time not at Moroseta, but instead a frequent visitor to Openhouse's events in Barcelona. Martino di Napoli Rampolla is a young graphic design graduate whose family owns a winery and a magnificent centuries-old building in the center of Florence. He approached Trotter with an idea of turning Numeroventi into a space that, like Openhouse, invited people in to create and view art, to come together and share ideas.

"Usually the places where you stay in Florence are very heavy or too modern, so we wanted something very light and calm." As consultant on the project, Trotter helped di Napoli Rampolla determine what to do with the space and how to fill it. Numeroventi blends white walls with characterful historic frescoes and vintage furniture, offering apartments for rent and hosting an artist residency program. Although it's in the city center, you feel like you're miles away.

Trotter visits Masseria Moroseta on a near monthly basis, especially in the winter when the space is quiet and calls for sitting by the fire and gazing over the sea. He comes here to work, because in the tranquility and dry breeze he can keep a clear head and focus. Among the projects he's working on is a house of his own. "I'm going to build my house next door to Masseria Moroseta because I want the same feeling." After living in five places in three countries, it's here among the olive trees in Puglia that Trotter—now a burgeoning architect as well as an established designer and art director—has finally found a place to settle down.

Sicilian Sanctuary

←
This home was built in the
1800s and was originally
an olive mill and animal
stables.

↑
The living room's fireplace
is set into a circular depression in the floor—the place
where the former millstone
pressed the olives.

This home is nestled deep in the eastern Sicilian landscape, an area that
shimmers with heat and smells of sage and thyme. The owners of this country retreat, Ausilia di Natale and Fabio Lentini, believe, "It was the house
that chose us." Built in the late 1800s, and originally an olive oil mill and
animal stables, it uses raw stone wall topped with a double-pitch roof, which
the designers Valentina Giampiccolo and Giuseppe Minaldi combined with
stained wood and a concrete floor. Its minimalist aesthetic includes a new
wood loft built using traditional methods. The mill's living room floor has
a circular depression where the millstone that pressed olives was previously
situated. Above, a large chimney with a conical flute is a feature piece. The
kitchen's iron and concrete island block has a stove and sink, while the east-
facing dining room contains a rectory table, color popping beneath with red
and blue chairs. Duck-egg blue French doors offset the pale pink natural stone;
they lead outside to the guesthouse, where Sicily's ambient silence awaits.

← ↑ →
Raw stone wall is combined
with stained wood and a
concrete floor in the kitch-
en, as well as an iron and
concrete island block with
a stove and sink.

↗
The east-facing dining room
has a rectory table complete
with colorful chairs, while
French doors lead outside to
the guesthouse.

The bedroom is sparsely
furnished with a minimal
side table, vintage stool, and
simple linens upon the bed.

Topanga Home | Topanga, California, USA | Design by Mason St Peter and Serena Mitnik-Miller

California Dreaming

Light fills this Californian living space, which was built in 1927 as a hunting lodge. Its open-plan kitchen and living room are defined by a mix of white walls and wooden furnishings, clerestory windows and skylights filling it with light. The roof rafters and paneled ceiling are also whitewashed, while the flooring is very pale pink natural wood. Interior designer Mason St Peter renovated his home together with his partner, Serena Mitnik-Miller. "The scope of this project was to take an existing home, strip it back to it's core, and carefully build it back up with a minimal amount of materials and volumes to achieve a light-filled living space with an indoor/outdoor connection," St Peter says. The internal garden brings together a mix of plants, many of which also grow in the warm climes of the Mediterranean. The kitchen was built by Ian Eichelberger and Michael Beavers custommade the furniture, while the kitchen's assortment of Japanese plates and bowls come from a variety of flea markets and L.A.'s Tortoise General Store.

← ↑
This former hunting lodge
has an open-plan living
room and kitchen, which
is filled with light from
clerestory windows and
skylights, complemented by
warm wooden furnishings
and an indoor garden.

↑
A Paul McCobb-style shelf houses a small library, which can be appreciated from an Eames chair.

←
A wood sculpture of an open-palm hand rests on a Paul McCobb coffee table.

↗
Japanese plates and bowls
fill the kitchen shelves,
sourced in flea markets and
L. A.'s Tortoise General Store.

→
The bedroom's natural wood
flooring is offset by whitewashed roof rafters and
a paneled ceiling.

Easy Like Sunday Morning

The windows of this house look out onto picturesque views of oak and cedar trees set into the Texan landscape. It is not surprising that Sunday House is named after the most relaxing day of the week. Its white interiors are offset with key wooden features, not least original roof beams, which are exposed through the open-plan living room and kitchen. Designer Kate Zimmerman Turpin wanted a simple, soft, and natural finish, enabling the house to seamlessly resonate with the surrounding environment. Inside, a deep ceramic sink is the keystone around which kitchen cabinets have been built, white coldness contrasting with the porous warmth of wood. Accompanied by a built-in bookcase and seating integrated into the walls, the living area sits next to giant glass doors that frame the scenery. A nude wooden doorframe leads into a minimally elegant bedroom, where the bed faces the window: the perfect wake-up call. This room's walk-in shower and bathroom reflect the philosophy of the house: one of light, air, and openness. Injections of color come through rugs and cushions dotted throughout—textiles that add dashes of warmth and vibrancy to this calm haven.

←
Oak and cedar trees are visible beyond the metalwork doors, resting in the Texan landscape.

↑
The open-plan kitchen-living room has original roof beams accompanied by a simple and natural finish that uses pale, neutral textiles.

→

←
The living room area has built-in shelving and seating that integrates into the walls.

↑
The bedroom combines long flowing linen curtains with a simple, wooden folding chair, woven rug, and neutral bedspread.

↑
The small house comprising
the bedroom of this ware-
house home is made from
maple wood.

→
The woven objects displayed
upon the wall, from fans
to bags and bowls, were
collected on the couple's
travels around the world.

Russian-Doll Warehouse

Leah Hudson-Smith designed her Melbourne home to have a Russian-doll effect: houses within houses. An interior designer with extensive experience working with architecture firms, Hudson-Smith's vast warehouse has typical industrial features including a concrete floor and high windows, within which architectural interventions include a charcoal-colored house that functions as a music studio for her partner, Wally Maloney, as well as a small house made of maple wood that they use as a bedroom. Hudson-Smith says, "I wanted a raised insulated floor and pitched roof for passive thermal control, [creating] a cozy place to fall asleep in our own adult-size cubby house." This home is filled with treasures collected from the couple's travels, from the rugs and natural textiles hanging on the walls to the trinkets, artworks, and books that tell the stories of their international adventures. Hudson-Smith's furniture company Pono connects art, design, and making—and here in her home, the bed, coffee tables, dining table, and plant stands dotted throughout the space are all made according to her own designs.

Northcote 2-in-1 Warehouse

|←
The original industrial features of this space include the poured-concrete flooring and high windows, with the dining table and plant stands made according to Hudson-Smith's own designs.

←
Tall bar stools in the kitchen tuck under the breakfast nook.

Schoolhouse Loft | New York City, USA | Design by Space Exploration

School's Out

↑ →
The open-plan kitchen-
dining room has cabinetry
by Henrybuilt and a vintage
Garland commercial stove.
The abstract artwork and
ceramic vases in the dining
room are framed by plants
and pendant lighting.

Beneath the soaring ceilings of a converted school building in south
Williamsburg, an airy, minimal home has taken form. The latest iteration
undos the building's long history of piecemeal renovations into a cohesive
interior, defined by its clean white walls, bold black details, and earth-hued
accents. Despite the challenges faced by the architects–an awkward column
grid, a very long project lifespan and budget constraints–one thing was
clear: this historic home, its big windows, and high ceilings had immense
potential. The breezy space is furnished to the taste of the owners, who have
a soft spot for the louche proportions of 1970s furniture. Tactile textures like
linens, woven rugs, and timber give the home a comfortable, crafted feel, but
perhaps its biggest success is its seeming simplicity. What the interior does
not reveal is that the kitchen took multiple iterations, and that the floor plan
needed rethinking to accommodate the arrival of one and then another new
baby. But the resulting space, which celebrates its period details in a contemporary context, is an effortless interior that was well worth the effort.

↑
The massive main bedroom
has an adjacent main bath
and dressing room.

→
Sofas from CB2 have a
built-in appearance because
of a corner table and
textured cushions. The over-
sized paper pendant light
and small table lamp are
both from the Akari collection by Isamu Noguchi.

Schoolhouse Loft

A

Alan Chu
Brazil
chu.arq.br
Ap Cobogó (pp.92–93)
Photos: Djan Chu

AnahoryAlmeida
Portugal
anahoryalmeida.com
Photo: Inês d'Orey
(p. 73 bottom right)

Andrew Trotter (Profile)
Spain & Italy
andrew-trotter.com
Photos: Salva Lopez (p. 72 top
left, 101 top, 252–255, 256 bottom),
Marcelo Martinez (p. 251), Marina
Denisova (p. 256 top, 257, 258–259)

Anna Malmberg
Sweden
annamalmbergphoto.com
Photos: (pp. 37 top, 63–64, 100,
153, 157 bottom right)

AOO
Spain
aoobarcelona.com
Photos: Jara Varela
(pp. 107 bottom, 109 top right)
Salvador Chair, designed by
Miguel Mila for AOO

Architetti Artigiani Anonimi
Italy
architettiartigianianonimi.com
Casa Kastellorizo (pp. 222–227)
Photos: Filippo
Bamberghi/Photofoyer

Arnaud Mauriers and Eric Ossart
Morocco
ossart-maurieres.com
Sidi ou Sidi (pp. 228–235)
Photos: Ricard Romain

Atelier Studios
Australia
instagram.com/atelier_studios
Photos: Maree Homer (pp. 150–151)

Atelier Vime
France
ateliervime.com
Photos: Anthony Watson/Atelier
Vime (pp. 99, 102 top, 104,
108 top left and right, 109 top left
and bottom left)

B

BFGF
USA
bfgf-shop.com
Photo: Daniel McKee (p. 34)

C

Caroline Feiffer
Denmark
instagram.com/carolinefeiffer
Home of Caroline Feiffer
(pp. 246–249)
Photos: Katrine Rohrberg
Caroline Engell Feiffer:
designer, home owner and
stylist of the images

Cobalto Studio
Spain
cobaltostudio.com
The Apartment of Gabriel Escámez
(pp. 12–15)
Photos: Pablo Zamora

Colapso Studio
Spain
colapsostudio.com
Workplace and Apartment
(pp. 172–173)
Photos: Elton Rocha

Couleur Locale
Belgium
couleurlocale.eu
Photos: Jeltje Janmaat (pp. 4, 147)

Cuffhome
USA
cuffstudio.com
The Dell (pp. 166–167)
Photos: Daniel Hennessy

D

DZEK
UK
dzekdzekdzek.com
Photo: Courtesy of Dzek (p.70)
ExCinere by Dzek in collaboration
with Formafantasma

E

Emmanuel Picault
Mexico
chic-by-accident.com
Santa Catarina House (pp. 128–133)
Photos: Javier Salas

Ezz Wilson
USA
ezzwilson.com
Photos: Ezz Wilson (pp. 152 top,
154, 156 top right)

F

Faye Toogood
UK
fayetoogood.com
Casa Paloma (pp. 54–57)
Photos: Tobias Alexander Harvey

Festen Architecture
France
festenarchitecture.com
Les Roches Rouges (pp. 85–87)
Photos: Nicole Franzen

Fornace Brioni
Italy
fornacebrioni.it
Photos: Mattia Balsamini (pp. 71 top,
72 bottom left, 73 centre left)
Design and Art Direction by
Cristina Celestino

G

Granby Workshop
UK
granbyworkshop.co.uk
Photo: GRANBY (pp. 71 bottom)

OOAK Architects
Sweden
ooakarchitects.com
Patio House (pp. 46 – 49, 68 – 69)
Photos: Yiorgos Kordakis

P

Paloma Wool
Spain
palomawool.com
Home of designer Paloma Lanna
(pp. 94 – 97, 102 bottom)
Photos: Cesar Segarra

Pampa—Rugs and Objects
Australia
pampa.com.au
Photos: Victoria Aguirre
(pp. 30 bottom, 31 bottom, 32 top,
33, 36 top left and bottom left,
149 bottom)

Pietro Cuevas
Spain
Can Xic (pp. 134 – 137)
Photos: Nicola Carignani/Photofoyer

R

Re-act Architects
Greece
re-act.gr
Maison Kamari (pp. 50 – 53,
157 bottom left)
Photos: Damien de Medeiros

Robert McKinley
USA
robertmckinley.com
McKinley Bungalow
(pp. 168 – 171, 103 top, 108 bottom
left)
Photos: Nicole Franzen

S

Sarah Ellison (Profile)
Australia
sarahellison.com.au
Photos: Dave Wheeler (pp. 74 – 79)

Sarah and Grégoire Rasson
Morocco
instagram.com/riad42marrakech
Riad 42 (pp. 192 – 197)
Photos: Britney Gill Photography

Serge Castella (Profile)
Spain
sergecastella.com
Photos: Yves Duronsoy (p.111),
Manolo Yllera (pp.112 – 119)

Silent Living
Portugal
silentliving.pt
Casa No Tempo (pp. 198 – 203)
Photos: James Florio (p. 198, 199,
200 top left and bottom, 201), Nelson
Garrido (p. 202), Nikolay Ivanov
(p. 200 top right, 203)
Santa Clara 1728 (pp. 72 – 73)
Photos: Renée Kemps (72 bottom
right,), Alex Reyto (73 bottom left)

Sophie Alda
UK
sophiealda.co.uk
Photo: Sophie Alda (p. 152 bottom)

Space Exploration
USA
spaceexplorationdesign.com
Schoolhouse Loft (pp. 148, 280 – 283)
In collaboration with Staci Dover
Design
Photos: Nicole Franzen

Studio Gameiro
Portugal
studiogameiro.com
Photos: Tiago Casanova (p. 66)

Studio Gum
Italy
studiogum.it
Casa Farfaglia (pp. 260 – 267)
Photos: Filippo
Bamberghi/Photofoyer

T

Taller Héctor Barroso
Mexico
tallerhectorbarroso.com
Entre Pinos (pp.120 – 124)
Photos: Rory Gardiner

The Citizenry
USA
the-citizenry.com
Photos: The Citizenry
(pp. 106, 107 top)

The Dharma Door
Australia
thedharmadoor.com.au
Photos: Jessie Prince (pp. 149 top,
155 top, 156 top left,
157 top right)

The Home Project
Portugal
the-home-project.com
Casa Modesta (pp. 65, 67, 157 top
left, 206 – 211)
Photos: Alex Reyto
Architecture and furniture design:
PAr. Plataforma de Arquitectura

The Rug Trade
UK
therugtrade.com
Photos: Ola Smit (pp. 29, 31 top)
All rugs designed by Ella Jones
Styling and Art Direction by
Ana Kerin

Tigmi Trading
Australia
tigmitrading.com
Photos: Alicia Taylor (p. 35 top),
Bridget Woods (p.36 top right),
Kaitlin Liemandt (p.37 bottom right)

W

Willem Smit
Morocco
willem-smit.com
Villa Mabrouka (pp. 38 – 45)
Photos: Courtesy of Willem Smit

Working Holiday Studio
USA
workingholidaystudio.com
Casa Mami (pp. 158 – 161)
Photos: Candida Wohlgemuth

●

The New Mediterranean:
Homes and Interiors Under
the Southern Sun

This book was conceived, edited, and designed by gestalten.

Edited by Robert Klanten and Andrea Servert
Preface, profile and feature texts by Eliora Stuhler
Project descriptions by Louisa Elderton
Editorial Management by Lars Pietzschmann
Cover and Design by Anastasia Genkina
Layout by Anastasia Genkina and Stefan Morgner

Typefaces: Rotis Serif STD and Rotis Semi Serif STD
by Otl Aicher
Cover image by Jeltje Janmaat for coleurlocale.eu
Backcover images:
Top left: Torre Vedra, Elsa Young/Frank Features.
Top right: Villa Mabrouka, courtesy of Willem Smit.
Bottom left: Casa Kastellorizo, Filippo Bamberghi/Photofoyer.
Bottom right: Laurence Leenaert, courtesy of LRNCE

Printed by Printer Trento s.r.l., Trento, Italy
Made in Europe

Published by gestalten, Berlin 2019
6th printing, 2022

ISBN 978-3-89955-981-1

© Die Gestalten Verlag GmbH & Co. KG, Berlin 2019

All rights reserved. No part of this publication may be
reproduced or transmitted in any form or by any means,
electronic or mechanical, including photocopy or any
storage and retrieval system, without permission in writing
from the publisher.

Respect copyrights, encourage creativity!

For more information, and to order books, please visit
www.gestalten.com.

Bibliographic information published by the Deutsche
Nationalbibliothek. The Deutsche Nationalbibliothek lists
this publication in the Deutsche Nationalbibliografie;
detailed bibliographic data is available online at www.dnb.de

None of the content in this book was published in exchange
for payment by commercial parties or designers; gestalten
selected all included work based solely on its artistic merit.

This book was printed on paper certified according
to the standards of the FSC®.

MIX
Paper from
responsible sources
FSC® C015829